May, 1981

Dear Father Bill,

I pray that this gift of my book will be a blessing in your Priestly life. Larrod will know you, too, when I Know I have heard so many wonderful things about you... Then, Larrod & I share a mutual love for Bishley Helis. It seems like we, too, will share a mutual love for Richly Spranger!

May God continue to richly bless your ministry, this my prayer!

Yours in Christ,
Verla A. Morth

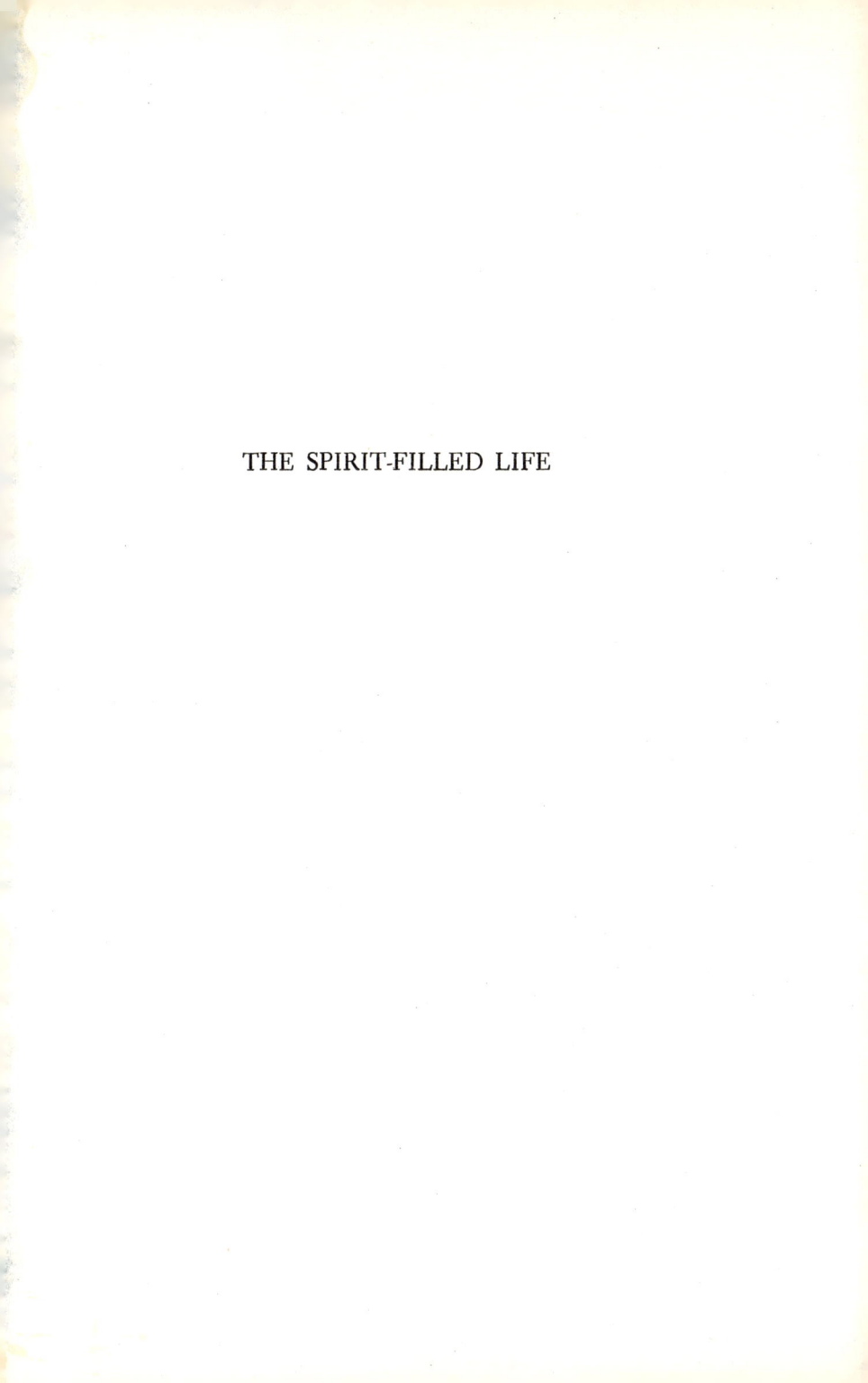

THE SPIRIT-FILLED LIFE

The Spirit-Filled Life

Verla A. Mooth

Exposition Press
Hicksville, New York

Scripture texts used in this work are taken from the *New American Bible*, copyright © 1970, by the Confraternity of Christian Doctrine, Washington, D.C., and are used by permission of the copyright owner. All rights reserved.

First Edition

© 1978 by Verla A. Mooth

All rights reserved, including the right of reproduction in whole or in part, in any form or by any means, electronic or mechanical, including photocopying, recording, or by any information storage and retrieval system. No part of this book may be reproduced without permission in writing from the publisher. Inquiries should be addressed to Exposition Press, Inc., 900 South Oyster Bay Road, Hicksville, N.Y. 11801

ISBN 0-682-49113-6

Printed in the United States of America

*To my beloved mother
in deep appreciation
for her wonderful example
of Spirit-filled living*

Contents

INTRODUCTION 9

1. Filled with the Spirit: What Does It Mean? 11
2. The Spirit of Holiness 20
3. Yielding to the Spirit 32
4. The Purifying Flame 39
5. The Person of the Spirit 49
6. The Spirit's Fullness 61
7. Power from on High 72
8. Filled with the Spirit—Led by the Spirit 83
9. The Laws of Fruit Bearing 91
10. The Fruit of the Spirit: Love 101
11. The Fruit of Joy and Peace 111
12. The Fruits of Endurance and Kindness 123
13. The Fruits of Generosity and Faith 133
14. The Fruits of Mildness and Chastity 142
15. The Spirit of Sacrifice 154
16. The Spirit of Praise 164

Introduction

A truly Spirit-filled life is like a poem and every day a well-writ line in harmonized aspirings and struggle, sobs and songs of praise, hope and near despair. It is the repeating beat of the contradictions accepted in well-adjusted living.

The poem of the Spirit-filled life does not come of well-chosen words but of ordered hearts under the stirring of great conflicts. It comes of faith that can find God in the thundering sea and in the singing brooks, in sunlight and in shadows.

It is not difficult to see the poetry of the snow-clad mountains, the fragrant wild rose, or the bird awing in a morning doused with sunshine. It is deep within the soul that the poetry sometimes comes hard. The dark shadows are difficult to reconcile with the bright hopes. The tears do not seem to rhyme with the dreams they have destroyed.

We think that the Spirit-filled life would be a song easily sung if we could have only pleasant things. But this is not true. The song would be a monotone, the poem dull and colorless, and the meter uninteresting if we had but happy words and joyful emotions.

People—erratic, discordant, unpredictable—are often hardest to include in the rhyme of the Spirit-filled life. It seems it would be so easy if all were kind, friendly, and easy to love, but they are not. They are good and bad, pleasant and unpleasant. They are friends and they are enemies, yet we cannot escape them.

If they do not become part of our poem it will be incomplete. Even in their contradictions and contrasts, God would have us love and include them all.

Even our religious experience must find beauty in the sharp contrasts of our lives and our emotions. Prayer and faith, hope and love would become dull without the varied tones of near desperation amid our devotion. The poem must use the whole of life by the grace of God, if it is to be filled with harmony and rhyme.

For holiness is harmony in motion, and harmony possesses a unique beauty and power. Holiness as a lifestyle brings harmony to the soul. Inner conflicts cease, inner guilt is removed, inner impulses are in harmony with outward ethics, inner peace brings calm to life, and inner purpose gives direction to the daily walk of the Spirit-filled Christian.

And, like a beautiful sonnet, the ultimate meaning—the compendium—is summed up in the final lines of the verse:

> Never again shall they know hunger or thirst, nor shall the sun or its heat beat down on them, for the Lamb on the throne will shepherd them. He will lead them to springs of life-giving water, and God will wipe every tear from their eyes. (Rev. 7:16-17)

For this is what the Spirit-filled life is all about!

1

Filled with the Spirit: What Does It Mean?

According to God's calendar, we are a privileged generation, for we live in the era of the outpoured Holy Spirit. This epoch is described by the prophet Joel in chapter 2. The twenty-eighth verse of that chapter climaxes the prophecy with the promise "I will pour out my spirit upon all flesh." Jesus promised this also, in John 14:16: "I will ask the Father and he will give you another Paraclete—to be with you always."

In describing the great event of Pentecost, Peter declares, "But this is that which was spoken by the prophet Joel" (Acts 2:16). Paul reminds us that this is a New Testament reality, in I Corinthians 3:16, "Are you not aware that you are the temple of God, and that the spirit of God dwells in you?" Again, in his letter to the Ephesians he admonished Christians to accept their heritage and "be filled with the Spirit" (Eph. 5:18).

To be filled with the Holy Spirit is the spiritual birthright of every believer. The very heart of the Pentecostal experience was that "all were filled with the Holy Spirit" (Acts 2:4). Being filled with the Spirit is the true norm of New Testament Christianity.

Being filled with the Spirit meets man's basic need. We are so constituted that we must be possessed by something or someone beyond ourselves. We are created by God to find our full completeness in Him. Without the fullness of the Spirit we are less than God intended us to be. This is what holiness is all about! The word *Holiness* simply means to be whole, to have a completeness in God.

Being "filled with the Spirit" is not a transitory experience but an abiding fullness, giving joy and power. It is the privilege of every child of God to be so possessed by the Spirit that he is endued with His power and fullness. For the fullness of the Spirit, rightly understood, is the active, growing, progressive experience of the pure in heart. And this leads us to three important questions: What does it mean to be filled with the Holy Spirit? Is not the Holy Spirit a person? How can one person fill another person? We read several times—especially in the book of Acts—about believers being filled with the Holy Spirit. What does it mean?

Luke tells us that on the Day of Pentecost the house where the disciples were gathered was filled with the Holy Spirit (Acts 2:2), and then he goes on to say that the disciples were filled with the Holy Spirit (Acts 2:4). Are men filled with the Holy Spirit the same way that a house is filled with wind? As we look closer, we find that Luke uses two different words, both translated "filled" in most English versions. In fact, every time Luke speaks of men being filled with the Holy Spirit (Acts 2:4;4:8,31;9:17;-13:9) he uses a special word. What does this word mean?

It is significant that at the Cross they filled a sponge with vinegar and gave it to Jesus (cf. Matt. 27:48), and here is the same word that Luke uses to describe being filled with the Spirit. A sponge is filled by soaking or saturating it. The sponge is permeated or penetrated, actually changing shape and size. By contrast, the house that is filled with wind simply receives the full capacity it can contain, like a glass that is filled with water. The house, or the glass, are unaffected by that with which they are filled—they are simply containers.

When we are filled with the Holy Spirit, it is more like the saturation of a sponge than the filling of a glass or container.

How else does Luke use this special word? He uses it to describe persons being filled with wrath (Luke 6:11), with wonder (Acts 3:10), with indignation (Acts 5:17), and with envy (Acts 13:45).

What does Luke mean by these vivid descriptions? It is more than a matter of these persons possessing these emotions, even to the fullest capacity. Instead these emotions possessed them. To be filled means to be controlled!

Filled with the Spirit: What Does It Mean?

Now we begin to understand what Luke means by being filled with the Holy Spirit. The Holy Spirit is a Person—God Almighty! He does not fill up our hearts like some impersonal substance filling a vessel. He comes and possesses us. *He takes control of us!* To speak of the Spirit-filled life is to speak of the Spirit-controlled life!

But doesn't Paul speak of being filled with the Spirit? Yes. The one instance is in Ephesians 5:18: "Avoid getting drunk on wine; that leads to debauchery. Be filled with the Spirit."

St. Paul does not use Luke's special word, but instead uses the common term that means to fill up a vessel with a substance. Nor does Paul use the crisis tense, as Luke always does, but instead is picturing a process. It is more in keeping with Paul's thoughts to understand him as saying: "Be filled *by* the Spirit— thus urging us to let the Holy Spirit fill us with His fruit (cf. Phil. 1:11; Gal. 5:22-23).

When Luke speaks of the believers being possessed and controlled by the Spirit, this marks the *entrance* upon a life of fellowship and companionship that Paul describes as walking or living by the Spirit (cf. Rom. 8:4-5; Gal. 5:16,25; Eph. 4:1;5:2,15).

Sometimes when we speak of being filled with the Holy Spirit (being full) we have the picture of an increase in quantity or amount. Some have said that we first get *part* of the Holy Spirit and then later *all* of the Holy Spirit in a second installment. It is not so much a matter of us getting more of the Spirit as it is the Spirit getting more of us, as we shall see later. Perhaps this *seems* as though we get more of Him.

The subsequence or secondness of the Spirit-filled life, which is designated by "Birth of the Spirit" and "Baptism with the Spirit" is best understood in terms of a *deeper control* rather than of a second coming of the Spirit in an additional amount.

When the newborn child of God takes the new life that he has received and *returns* it to God in total consecration (cf. Rom. 6:13;12:1), the Holy Spirit takes control of his life in a new and deeper way.

It is impossible for the Spirit to be sovereign as long as sin remains in the believer's heart. We can't be sovereign and the

Holy Spirit be sovereign at the same time! But, in response to our full commitment, the sin is removed from our hearts and the Spirit *possesses* or *controls* us as Lord.

So—what does it mean to be filled with the Spirit? It means to have our lives under the control of the Spirit! There is a moment of crisis when the Spirit takes control of our lives in response to our total commitment, which Luke describes in Acts. But such is only the *entrance* to a life under the control of the Spirit as we walk in fellowship with Him.

As we live under the control of the Spirit and walk in companionship with Him, there is victory over sin (cf. Gal. 5:16). Beyond that there stretches the endless horizon of spiritual conquest. "To him whose power now at work in us can do immeasurably more than we ask or imagine—to him be glory in the church and in Christ Jesus through all generations, world without end. Amen" (Eph. 3:30-31).

Chapter 5 of Ephesians also provides some interesting insight into the blessedness of the indwelling Spirit: First, the Holy Spirit brings a cleansing to the soul. The soul is cleansed to "follow the way of love, as Christ also has loved us" (verse 2); and "Lewd conduct or promiscuousness or lust of any sort let them not even be mentioned among you; your holiness forbids this" (verse 3). The Holy Spirit enables us to "keep careful watch over your conduct. Do not act like fools, but like thoughtful men" (verses 15-16).

The indwelling Spirit brings also a spiritual illumination into the soul. "There was a time when you were darkness but now you are light in the Lord. Well, then, live as children of light" (verse 8). This inner illumination produces a spiritual sensitivity to "discern the will of the Lord" (verse 17). The indwelling Holy Spirit gives the soul an inner quality of tenderness. Verse 21 says, "Defer to one another out of reverence to Christ." In verses 22-25 this quality become the basis of happy relationships, and indeed of all our ethical obligations. It is reflected in daily conduct, in attitudes, in words spoken, and in all our private and public relationships. It further produces a conviction "to make the most of the present opportunity" (verse 16).

The indwelling Spirit becomes our source of inner gladness and joy. Verse 19 tells us, "Addressing one another in psalms and hymns and inspired songs. Sing praise to the Lord with all your heart." This is a blessed state of the soul which enables the Christian to follow the admonition in verse 20, "Give thanks to God the father always and for everything in the name of Our Lord Jesus Christ."

When the Holy Spirit lives in a person, the life of that person takes on a new dimension—the ability to put into effect the right intentions and desires. Peter loved his Master so much that he really did intend to give his life in defense of Jesus if necessary. But when faced with the opportunity of identifying himself as a follower of Jesus, he failed; he denied his Lord. What was the reason for Peter's inadequacy? Why did he fail? *He had not yet received the Holy Spirit, the Enabler, the divine helper.* But Pentecost made for Peter all the difference!

Today many followers of Jesus are caught in the same dilemma as Peter—high and holy desire regularly matched with failure and defeat when there ought to be victory. So, just as Peter found the full, adequate, and personal answer to his "failure problem" in the empowering presence of the Holy Spirit, so must every believer accept and live by Jesus' promise to His disciples as recorded in John 14:16. The one who leaves all to follow Jesus must be enabled by the Holy Spirit to live out in his own life the example set by Jesus in this earthly life.

When the Holy Spirit comes in His powerful presence, some things thought to be impossible from any purely human point of view become possible. No man in his own strength can fulfill the greatest of the commandments, that is, to love as Jesus loved (John 13:34). How did He love? It was a love that excluded no person—not even Nicodemus, Mary Magdalene, Judas, or Simon the outcast leper.

Most of the failures of the Christian who is not Spirit-filled can be traced to an unfulfilled desire to love as Jesus loves His Father, His disciples, His friends, His enemies, and properly His own self. Who has not said, "I can't stand that person"? Or even felt at times that they could not stand themselves. Are there not always some interpersonal relations that seem to be inevitably characterized by anything but love? It is only by receiving the fullness of the Holy Spirit that the impossible becomes possible—to be able to love as Jesus loved!

When we are born into the kingdom of God, we are not much to look at as Christians. We are uninformed in spiritual things, and we are weak and helpless. The apostle Paul called newly born Christians "babes in Christ—weak and immature." Yet the Lord sees what we can become, so He gives to us His Holy Spirit to help us along the way.

Jesus impressed upon the disciples the fact that the presence of the Holy Spirit spells the difference between spiritual success and failure: "Remain here in the city, until you are clothed with power from on high" (Luke 24:49).

Why is His presence so necessary? Every promise in the Bible presupposes a need, a demand for which the promise is made. There is a demand in every person for the Spirit of God. "My heart and my flesh crieth out for the living God" (Ps. 84:2).

We were created to be God's home. "You must know that your body is a temple of the Holy Spirit, who is within—the Spirit you have received from God" (1 Cor. 6:19). These words of Paul suggest that "you must know you are meant to be, you are created to be God's home in whom He is to live!"

The manner in which the Spirit came into the lives of those on the Day of Pentecost—as "a mighty wind rushing"—is not insignificant. He rushed into their lives as one eager to possesss the building designed to be His home. As soon as the door was open—He was in! So quickly—so easily—so effortlessly!

Each of us is possessed by some kind of spirit (cf. Eph. 5:18). What kind of a spirit fills me, possesses, controls me? An unholy spirit of jealousy, fear, timidity, resentment, doubting? That unholy spirit is dissipation. The Holy Spirit is health to the whole person. Jesus said, "Receive the Holy Spirit." Every demand of the spirit, mind, soul, and body will be met by His grace!

God's self-revelation climaxed in Jesus' life, death, and resurrection; His self-impartation climaxed in His coming through the Spirit at Pentecost to indwell and sanctify His people. Jesus

Filled with the Spirit: What Does It Mean?

is God *with* us; the Holy Spirit is God *in* us. God's call to holiness of heart and life, without which no man shall see Him, is not a call to any particular denomination or movement. It is, however, an indispensable requirement that all children of God be Spirit-filled Christians if they are to attain the fullness of their vocation in Christ.

There is no way to minimize the "secondness" of a personal Pentecost. For, moving "on from grace to grace," the marked change from self-sovereignty to Spirit-sovereignty in the trusting, obedient child of God is indeed a crisis subsequent to regeneration, in exactly the same way that the Sacrament of Confirmation is subsequent to the Sacrament of Baptism.

The latter denotes the Spirit's work in conversion and regeneration, by which He makes sinners members of Christ and His Church under the seal of water baptism.

The baptism with the Spirit is something different. It is a gift given by Christ to those who by the Spirit have been incorporated into Christ's Body, the Church. Our Lord baptizes them with His Spirit, pouring the Spirit out upon them. He fills them with the Spirit, thus granting them power from on high for witness and Christian service. *This baptism with the spirit may truly be called a "sharing in the Pentecostal blessing."*

Historically, Pentecost can never be repeated. Personally, and spiritually it becomes a living reality for all who present their bodies as living sacrifices in unreserved consecration to God (Rom. 12:1-2). *The Spirit fills only emptied vessels! God empowers only those He can control!*

One of the reasons why many fail to recognize the Biblical doctrine of post-conversion baptism with the Holy Spirit is certainly to be found in the fact that in the New Testament this Spirit baptism is mentioned under different names.

The phrase "baptized with the Holy Spirit" occurs only once in the New Testament after Pentecost. This is in reference to the "Caesarean Pentecost," when Cornelius and his family were filled with the Spirit (Acts 11:16).

When the promise of Jesus was fulfilled, as it was in the events recorded in Acts 2, Luke speaks of the disciples as being "filled with the Spirit" (verse 4). "Filled with the Spirit" thereafter becomes the normal way of speaking about the results of the "baptism with the Spirit."

In the Christian experience there is nothing more important than the baptism with the Holy Spirit. We are aware that, in the broadest sense, sanctification includes the whole Christian experience, from regeneration to glorification. In a narrow sense, however, the term *sanctification*—or *purification*—is also used in referring to the purification that is the specific work of the Cleansing Flame of the Holy Spirit (cf. Matt. 3:11). It is the Holy Spirit who gives the power to live a victorious and fruitful Christian life.

The outstanding writer on the Holy Spirit, Rev. A.B. Simpson, states: "There is an infinite difference between this reception of the Holy Spirit and His coming to us at our conversion. There He comes to witness to our acceptance and forgiveness; here He comes to accept our perfect offering of ourselves to Him, and to possess us fully for Himself, bringing us into personal union with Jesus, and keeping us henceforth in obedience and victory."

We take it for granted that all of us understand that before entering into the positive side of the baptism with the Holy Spirit there must have been proper preparation made—that is, an acceptance and embracing of the Cross of Calvary. This cannot be overemphasized. Full surrender to God, faith in the blood to cleanse from sins, and faith in the Cross to cleanse from inner sinfulness are of the utmost importance if one desires to be a candidate for the baptism with the Holy Spirit.

That there is some misunderstanding and objection to using the term "baptism with the Holy Spirit," we are well aware. But this is not to be, as we have said, confused with the indwelling of the Holy Spirit in the "Birth of the Spirit." The Holy Spirit *indwells* every Christian who has been genuinely regenerated, enabling him to live a victorious life; but the Holy Spirit *comes upon* or *is given* to us in the baptism with the Spirit in order to purify, fill, and empower for effective service. The *life* of a Christian begins at the Cross; his *service* begins at Pentecost!

There is, indeed, no contradiction at all between having the

Filled with the Spirit: What Does It Mean?

Holy Spirit as the same Spirit of repentance, faith, and regeneration, and at the same time standing in need of the baptism with the Spirit promised to believers.

One could put it as follows: The Lord grants His Spirit first to sinners, to bring them into a living relationship with Himself and the Church, by granting them faith and a new life under the seal of water baptism. But then Christ is ready to baptize them with the Spirit, i.e., to fill them experientially with the same Spirit. He is ready to do so in order that these members, His Body, should be fully cleansed, filled, and equipped to render Christian service to their Saviour, to one another, and to the world around them.

A personal Pentecost, then, represents normal and vitally real Christianity. The Holy Spirit "glorifies" Christ. The most natural step imaginable is for the person who has received eternal life as the gift of God to receive the gift of the Holy Spirit, *which was Christ's parting gift to His people.*

We want to state clearly that we know every Christian *has* the Holy Spirit. But at the same time, we also know that every Christian is not *filled* with the Spirit. As T. A. Hegre states, in his book *The Cross and Sanctification,* "To have the Holy Spirit 'resident' is a different thing from having Him 'president'—by which we mean, the experience (available for every Christian) of being Spirit-filled, Spirit-controlled, and Spirit-empowered."

In the words of William Barclay, "The drabness of life, and the inadequacy of life, and the futility of life, and the earth-boundness of life, which characterizes so many of us, all come from the failure to submit to the baptism of the Spirit which Christ alone can give!"

2

The Spirit of Holiness

To be made holy is to be made like Jesus. He sanctifies us by reproducing His own life in ours. As we have already stated, holiness begins with regeneration, with the marvelous experience of being born again. For, in the new birth, the life of the Risen Jesus is communicated to us. We become alive spiritually, alive with His life.

The Christ-life is given to make us Christlike. It must come to expression inside of us and outside of us. It must govern our thinking, our intentions, our decision making. And it must govern what we say and do, hallowing every relationship we bear to others, in our homes, on our jobs, at our schools, in our business—wherever life touches life.

The life of Jesus in us cannot come to its desired expression unless the poisoned source of our old way of life is destroyed. The self-centeredness, the god-playing "I" from which our sins of word and deed emerge, must be crucified. A deep inner cleansing must occur that will make life a circle with one Center, Jesus, rather than an ellipse with two foci, Jesus and "I."

The holiness begun with the new birth demands that our hearts be sanctified wholly, The Christ-life must be released to flow unchecked and unpolluted. There must be "love out of a pure heart," to borrow a phrase from the Apostle Paul.

The full and clear expression of the Christ-life is not only hindered by indwelling sin, however, but also by the failures and blunders that are traceable to our fallen and infirm humanity. Damaging things are sometimes done, not because our hearts are wrong, but because our minds function so imperfectly. We have this treasure in a vessel of clay. This means that, in addition to the experience of cleansing that occurs in a moment of faith, there must be discipline and growth throughout a lifetime

The Spirit of Holiness

of faithfulness. When we discover anything in our attitudes and actions inconsistent with the Christ-life, we must change.

For this reason we never get beyond the need of renewed forgiveness and cleansing. There is a daily sanctification of life requried of Christians who would become increasingly like Jesus.

The new birth, the cleansing of entire sanctification, and the constant examination, discipline, and pruning of our lives are all included in the process by which Jesus makes His life in us become His likeness in us.

It is the prerogative of God, through the Holy Spirit, to apply the merits of Christ's atonement and make us clean vessels. Our role is to be available to Him.

Jesus gave Himself to purify us unto Himself "a peculiar people, zealous of good workers." God reminded Israel, "For you are a people sacred to the Lord, your God. He has chosen you from all the Nations on the face of the earth to be a people peculiarly His own" (Deut. 7:6). But being "peculiarly His own people" does not mean being a weird people!

What God provided for ancient Israel he has available for the New Israel, the Church. His own people He has called to be peculiarly His own. Some have interpreted the description to mean "isolated" or "insulated" from the world. This view is inconsistent with Jesus' prayer in John 17:15: "I do not ask you to take them out of the World, but to guard them from the evil one."

The term "peculiarly His own" as used here means "special." Two things made Israel special: their love for Yahweh and their concern for each other. In a unique way ancient Israel was a "classless" society. Yet each person, however lowly, was of equal value before God. God had called them to be His holy people. They were a race apart. 1 Peter 2:9 further states: "You however, are, a chosen race, a royal priesthood, a holy nation, a people he claims for his own to proclaim the glorious works. Of the one who called you from darkness into marvelous light" (cf. Isa. 43:20-21).

Vocation and choice belong to the essence of God's plan of salvation and its realization in human history. Bound up with vocation is the idea of the Alliance, in which the religion of the

Old and New Testament finds its essential expression. The Scriptures define holiness not merely as a separation from the profane, but, more profoundly, in terms of the revelation of God in His activity and choice. Sanctity is the mystery of God Himself and His communication with men. *This mystery is revealed in all its splendor in the gift of the Spirit of-holiness dwelling in the hearts of men, and manifested in the* charity of Christ, which distinguishes them as holy people (cf. John 13:25).

As the Holy One, God dwelt among the Israelites to sanctify His people (cf. Exod. 29:45-46). As the Holy One, He dwells in us. It is the presence of God alone that can sanctify. But so surely is this our portion, that Scripture does not shrink from speaking of God dwelling in our hearts in such power that we may be "filled unto all the fulness of God." True holiness is fellowship with God and His dwelling in us. So it was necessary that God in Christ should take up His abode in the flesh, and the Holy Spirit should come to dwell in us.

The truth of the body as a temple of God is one of Christ's major revelations. As a boy He had called the temple in Jerusalem "my Father's house," the earthly house of the eternal and heavenly King. There God revealed himself, and there men communed with and worshipped Him. Even so, God has always wanted to make His home in His people and to live and walk in them. Isaiah, too, spoke of the high and lofty One who dwells not only in the high and holy place but *"with the crushed and dejected in spirit"* (Isa. 57:15). The Apostle Paul attested further to this truth when he reminded the Corinthians, "You must know that your body is a temple of the Holy Spirit, who is within you—the Spirit you have received from God" (1 Cor. 6:19).

Jesus' miraculous cleansing of the temple in Jerusalem, then, is a most beautiful and instructive figure of the cleansing of the temple of our physical bodies.

This miracle of the cleansing of the temple was a sign indicating Jesus' authority. "Destroy this temple," said Jesus, "and in three days I will raise it up" (that is, "I will resurrect it"). To all hearts who will give Christ permission, His resurrection life

The Spirit of Holiness

will come in with new love, with power, with grace, and with holiness, not only driving out the kingdom of darkness, but also setting up His new kingdom of grace. "And now, brothers, I beg you through the mercy of God to offer your bodies as a living sacrifice holy and acceptable to God, your spiritual worship" (Rom. 12:1). "Since we have these promises, beloved, let us purify ourselves from every defilement of flesh and spirit,, and in the fear of God strive to fulfill our consecration perfectly" (2 Cor. 7:1).

St. Paul's exhortation throughout his epistles to both the Colossians and the Ephesians is a call to righteousness—a casting off "the old man," to a "path of cleansing and continual progress."

This life lived in the fullness of the Spirit has been termed in classical theology as "sancity, holiness, or a deep spirituality." The word *spirituality* literally means "having the nature of spirit" or "having the nature of the Spirit." It means "Spiritlike." The Holy Spirit of God is the source of the spiritual man's discernment and quality of life.

This is the state of the Spirit-filled Christian in whom the flesh, the carnal nature, has been crucified. This is the end toward which all Christian teaching and exhortation should lead. God is vitally concerned not only with the redemption of natural men, but with the production of the spiritual man.

There is, perhaps, in all of Scripture no more explicit or urgent prayer for the continual progress or growth in the life of the Spirit than the one found in the Epistle of Paul the Apostle to the Colossians. St. Paul prays: "Ever since we heard this we have been praying for you unceasingly and asking that you may attain full knowledge of his will through perfect wisdom and spiritual insight. Then you will lead a life worthy of the Lord and pleasing to him in every way. You will multiply good works of every sort and grow in the knowledge of God. By the might of his glory you will be endowed with the strength needed to stand fast, even to endure joyfully whatever may come, giving thanks to the Father for having made you worthy to share the lot of the saints in light. He rescued us from the power of darkness and brought us into the kingdom of his beloved Son. Through him we have redemption, the forgiveness of our sins" (Col. 1:9-14).

In verses 21-23, St. Paul adds: "You yourselves were once alienated from him; you nourished hostility in your hearts because of your evil deeds. But now Christ has achieved reconciliation for you in his mortal body by dying, so as to present you to God holy, free of reproach and blame. But you must hold fast to faith, be firmly grounded and steadfast in it, unshaken in the hope promised you by the gospel you have heard. It is the gospel which has been announced to every creature under heaven, and I, Paul, am its servant."

The emphasis of the Scripture is that this holiness of heart and life of which Paul speaks involves three necessary elements: (1) obedience to the truth, (2) a life lived in complete faith and submission to the Holy Spirit, and (3) the divine gift of love.

On the eve of His crucifixion, Christ spoke of the new order—or Alliance—to be introduced at Pentecost.

> Anyone who loves me
> will be true to my word,
> and my Father will love him;
> we will come to him
> and make our dwelling place with him." (*John* 14:23)

Holiness is here defined as receiving the Comforter, the Spirit of truth, "whom the world cannot accept." Only the believer can accept the Spirit in His sovereign, sanctifying lordship. Holiness is not "a thing," and "it," an abstraction. Holiness is a Person, expelling sin from the heart by filling it with His love made perfect, a love that is not something apart from Him but His own nature.

Holiness in character and conduct is the fruit of the abiding fullness of the Holy Spirit. This means that it is a personal relationship between God the Giver and a human being as receiver.

Such an understanding at once banishes a dozen wrong ideas.

The Spirit of Holiness

Holiness is never something we work up to. It is a gift. It is not a "thing," some sort of heavenly substance. It is a quality derived from the Divine Presence.

Scripture teaches this in many ways. Jesus promised it:

> Anyone who loves me
> will be true to my word,
> and my Father will love him;
> we will come to him
> and make our dwelling place with him. *(John 14:23)*

Paul testifies to it: "And the life I live now is not my own; Christ is living in me. I still live my human life, but it is a life of faith in the Son of God, who loved me and gave himself for me" (Gal. 2:20).

Peter described it: "By virtue of them he has bestowed on us the great and precious things he promised, so that, through these, you who have fled a world corrupted by lust might become sharers of the divine nature" (2 Peter 1:4).

In each of these instances—and a score more that could be quoted—the same truth shines through. It is the Holy Spirit, the indwelling presence of Christ, making us partakers of God's own nature who is the *Key* to the sanctified life.

Here is no saccharine saintliness, no goody-goody pretense to piety. Here is the life more abundant (John 10:10). Here is the fullness of the blessing of the Gospel of Christ, which is the Spirit-filled life (Romans 15:29).

Many have seen this truth clearly. F. E. Marsh wrote, "We have no inherent holiness. We are holy as we are possessed by the holy Presence. We are holy in His holiness, loving in His love, strong in His strength, tender in His tenderness, patient in His patience, calm in His peace, and consecrated in His consecration. Get out of touch with Him by neglecting prayer, and the fragrance of His presence is wanting."

Commissioner Samuel Brengle of the Salvation Army wrote: "Do you want to know what Holiness is? It is pure love. Do you want to know what the Baptism of the Holy Ghost is? It is not mere sentiment. It is not a happy sensation that passes away in the night. It is a baptism of love that brings every thought into captivity to the Lord Jesus; that casts out all fear; that burns up doubt and unbelief as fire burns tow; that makes one hate uncleanness, lying and deceit, a flattering tongue, and every evil way with a perfect hatred; that makes Heaven and Hell eternal realities; that makes one patient and gentle with the froward and sinful; that makes one pure, peaceable, easy to be entreated, full of mercy and good fruits, without partiality and without hypocrisy; that brings one into perfect and unbroken sympathy with the Lord Jesus Christ in His toil and travail to bring a lost and rebel world back to God."

British Baptist Oswald Chambers—who, incidentally, has given Christianity some of its most penetrating insights into the life of holiness—wrote: "Holiness is not an attainment at all, it is a gift of God. The pietistic tendency is the introspection which makes me worship my own earnestness and not take the Lord seriously at all. It is a pious fraud that suits the natural man immensely. He makes holy. He sanctifies. He does it all. All I have to do is to come as a spiritual pauper, not ashamed to beg, to let go of my right to myself and act on Romans 12:1-2. It is never 'Do, Do' and you will be with the Lord, but 'Be, Be,' and I will *do* through you. It is a case of 'hands up' and letting go, and then entire reliance on Him."

If there is no holiness apart from the Holy Spirit, then our attitude toward, and openness to, the divine Comforter becomes all-important. The fruit of the Spirit is then seen to be the evidence of His holy abiding.

All the argument that has raged across the years about the possibility of a pure and holy heart must be judged in the light of the fact that the Spirit is *holy*. His concern is not with the psychological complexes and quirks. We shall have these in abundance until we enter the more excellent glory. His concern is with the basic motivations, the essential springs of life.

Even a qiuck glance at a Bible concordance shows the im-

The Spirit of Holiness

portance the writers of Scripture place upon what they call the "heart" of man. The Old Testament uses words for "heart" more than 800 times, and the New Testament 164 times.

While we tend to think of "heart" in terms of feeling, the Bible speaks of "heart" as the whole of the inner life. We not only love with our heart (Mark 12:30), we purpose in our hearts (Dan. 1:8), and we think with our hearts (Matt. 9:4).

God's first call to us is "Give me your heart." This is the first step into the Christian life—a call to trust, loyalty, and obedience. The result is loss of the "stony heart" of the unregenerated, and a "new heart" and a "new spirit" within (Ezek. 36:26).

But the scope of redemption does not stop with the impartation of life to a dead soul. Over and over, God calls His people to that grace the Scripture calls "a pure heart" or "a clean heart."

To "ascend to the mountain of the Lord" and "stand in his holy place" both in worship and in final destiny—demands "sinless hands, and a clean heart" (Ps. 23:3-4).

With a spiritual instinct greater than the light available in his day, the Psalmist prayed for a clean heart and a right spirit within (Ps. 51:10) and proclaimed God's special grace toward "those who are clean of heart" (Ps. 73:1). "Blessed are the single hearted," said Jesus, "for they shall see God" (Matt. 5:8).

Paul says that the goal of all God's commandments is love "that springs from a pure heart" (1 Tim. 1:5) and urges his young friend and helper to "turn from youthful passion and pursue integrity, faith, love, and peace, along with those who call on the Lord with purity of heart" (2 Tim. 2:22).

James echoes the words of Psalm 24:4, in the context of Christian experience, when he says, "Cleanse your hands, you sinners; and purify your hearts, you backsliders" (James 4:8).

As we have stated, for Peter the most memorable result of Pentecost in the lives of the disciples was that God gave the Holy Spirit, "purified their hearts by means of faith also" (Acts 15:8-9). In light of this, he later wrote, "By obedience to the truth you have purified yourselves for a genuine love of your brothers; therefore love one another constantly from the heart" (1 Peter 1:22).

The evidence is overwhelming. The question is, What does it mean to have a pure heart?

This question has an urgency for us it did not have for our fathers. We who live in the post-Freudian age have been told about the subconscious depths of personality in which are said to lurk motives and maladjustments of which we are never fully aware. We have been warned, in view of this, not to witness to a cleansing and inner healing of which we cannot be sure.

The warning has its point. But some things need to be said.

First, the Bible is not talking about a purity that would possibly satisfy the definitions of a depth psychologist. It is talking about a purity that satisfies the demands of a holy God.

When we talk about the grace of a pure heart, we do not necessarily mean what Freud would have meant—had he ever imagined such a possibility. We are talking about what God means by a pure heart.

Second, the words of Scripture do not depend for their validation on our powers of introspection. We cannot affirm that our hearts are pure in a scriptural sense because we do not detect defilement within.

But our position here is not different than is our position regarding the forgiveness of sins. We do not believe our sins are forgiven because we are able to scan the record in God's book of life and see that the page is clear. We believe our sins are forgiven because the Word declares,

> But if we acknowledge our sins,
> he who is just can be trusted
> to forgive our sins
> and cleanse us from every wrong.
> (Rom. 8:16)

In a similar way, we believe Spirit-filled hearts are pure because the Word declares,

The Spirit of Holiness

> But if we walk in light,
> as he is in the light,
> we have fellowship with one another,
> and the blood of his Son Jesus cleanses us
> from all sin.   (1 John 1:7)

If we would deny the need for such cleansing, John says, we "deceive ourselves; the truth is not to be found in us" (1 John 1:8).

And here, as in the witness of the Spirit to the new birth, multitudes of God's people have found that "the Spirit we have received is not the world's Spirit but God's Spirit, helping us to recognize the gifts he has given us" (1 Cor. 2:12).

Certainly "Christian perfection" includes no claim that Spirit-filled Christians are to become perfect individuals or even perfect Christians. *What it means is that the grace of God has brought them into a new and right relationship with a perfect Christ!*

In short, it is not our victory, it is always Christ's victory; it is never our work or holiness, it is always Christ's work and Christ's holiness. When we begin to think and to grow in the idea of our victory, there is really no true victory at all. To the extent the we are thinking about our sanctification, there is no real sanctification. We must see it always as Jesus Christ's.

Indeed, it is only as we consciously bring each victory to His feet, and keep it there as we think of it—and especially as we speak of it—that we can avoid the pride of that victory, which can be worse than the sin over which we claim to have had the victory. *The greater the victory the greater the need of placing it consciously at His feet.*

God's purpose, moreover, is to make us whole as human beings, not as angels in heaven. *Holiness* as an English word comes from a root meaning "whole." "Wholeness" is not our earning or contriving. It is the gift of grace in the sanctifying lordship of God's Holy Spirit in our hearts and lives.

Third, both in Scripture and in experience it is clear that a pure heart does not mean that all emotional tangles are straightened out, all maladjustments of personality or quirks of temperament are corrected, or all need for discipline and growth ended.

A pure heart may be immature, at times troubled, sorely tempted, tried as by fire. A pure heart does not necessarily mean a clear mind. We can walk in fellowship with God with wrong ideas in our head, but not with wrong attitudes in our hearts.

Negatively, a pure heart is one in which the inwardness of sin has been decisively dealt with by the grace of God. The deep-seated aversion of an unsanctified heart to the will of God has been corrected.

Sören Kierkegaard was very close to the full truth when he said, "Purity of heart is to will one thing." That one thing is the will of God.

Sin as a condition of the heart is basically being out of tune with God. In Morton Dorsey's unforgettable metaphor, when a violinist tunes the string to perfect pitch we do not wonder where the "out-of-tuneness" went. If the string later goes out of harmony, we do not puzzle over how the "out-of-tuneness" got back into the string.

Postively, and more importantly, a pure heart is a heart bathed in and filled with love. Never in a thousand years can we beat the darkness out of the cellar with a club. The way to deal with darkness is to let in the light!

If there has been any weakness in the traditional ways of presenting the doctrine of sanctity, it has been that we have too often stopped with the negative death of self and freedom from sin. These are real and precious. But there is more to holiness than the absence of sin, just as there is more to light than the absence of darkness.

A pure heart is one conditioned by the indwelling Spirit of Christ to love God with all the heart, soul, mind, and strength, and one's neighbor as himself. *Holiness is Christ reigning within, His love and His Spirit in control.*

This is the glorious fact of regeneration and sanctification: Not only does God renew man's moral image in which he was

The Spirit of Holiness

created, but, best of all, the Divine Sculptor Himself comes in the Person of the Holy Spirit and dwells within. He begins to remold the life from within. And no matter how broken by sins his previous life might have been—no matter how painfully scared the memories from the many hurts that have long been buried—His Spirit persists to save and heal to the uttermost. Through the coming of the Spirit, the alien is made friend, what was torn is made whole, what was wounded is healed!

In its simplest definition, holiness is Christlikeness begun and growing. It is the joy of belonging to a God greater than the crisis of the present.

In short, "holiness" and the "Spirit-filled life" are synonymous. They are but the two sides of the same coin!

3

Yielding to the Spirit

The human condition that marks the transition from the birth of the Spirit to the infilling with the Spirit is total self-surrender, or the consecration that only a child of God can make (Rom. 6:13-19; 12:1-2), a consecration that alone makes appropriating faith possible (Acts 26:18; Gal. 3:2,14).

The separation unto sanctification is always God's own work, and so the electing grace of God is often closely connected with sanctification (cf. Lev. 20:26; Num. 16:7; Deut. 7:6). God must be the sole possessor, and ruler, of those to whom He reveals and imparts His holiness.

But this separation is not all that is included in the word *sanctification*. It is preceded by and presupposes reconciliation, pardon, and cleansing from sin. Nor is the word *sanctfication* all that is included in the *Baptism with the Spirit*. It is only the indispensable condition for what must follow. When separated, man stands before God in no respect differing from an object without life that has been sanctified to service of God. If the separation is to be of value, something must take place. Man must surrender himself willingly, and heartily, to this separation. Sanctification includes *personal consecration* to the Lord.

The human side of holiness, therefore, is what is usually called "consecration, dedication, or full surrender." It is the bringing of a redeemed life and personality to be offered to God as a living sacrifice (Rom. 12:12).

The Bible itself relates consecration or separation to God with that which is holy. For example, "To me, therefore, you shall be sacred; for I the Lord, am sacred, I who have set you apart from the other Nations to be my own" (Lev. 20:26). Again, "You, however, are a chosen race, a royal priesthood, a holy Nation, a people he claims for his own to proclaim the glorious works of the One who called you from darkness into his marvelous light" (1 Peter 2:9).

It is rather easy to equate consecration with sanctification because they are so vitally related, and in some sense inseparable. But we must distinguish between them in order to avoid confusion. Actually, a full consecration is to sanctification what repentance is to justification. Before the sinner is converted, he must repent *and believe*. Likewise the believer must consecrate and believe in order to obtain the full blessing of Pentecost, the Baptism with the Holy Spirit.

Consecration, therefore, is the antecedent condition of sanctification, but not the thing itself. Consecration is man's work; sanctification is God's work. God never *consecrates* for us, and we never *sanctify* for God. It is true that the acts of consecration and sanctification are both combined in the work that produces the experience of holiness, yet they are forever separate and distinct. We consecrate; God sanctifies. We step on the altar; the blood cleanses.

Some modern translations of the Scriptures have used the words *consecration* and *sanctification* interchangeably. In general, however, the context of the Scriptures makes a distinction between the two. The emphasis of consecration is upon our commitment, whereas the connotation of sanctification is upon God's work or response to our commitment when faith is operative.

Scripture commentator Dr. H. Orton Wiley, is careful to point out, "The work of sanctification involves not only separation from sin, but a separation to God." *This positive devotement, he insists, "is something more than the human consecration of the soul to God. It represents, also, the Holy Spirit's acceptance of the offering, and therefore, a divine empowering or enduement."*

The great battleground for most Christians is in this matter of complete abandonment to the will of God. The struggle itself may be related to the clash with the carnal mind—the principle of evil that resides in the Christian due to the Fall. But there is an experience for us in which we can say an "eternal yes" to the will of God. This does not eliminate the daily "yes" as life's issues unfold from day to day, but it makes them relatively easy. Praise God!

The call to a crucial consecration must rest ultimately on the appeal of Calvary—"in view of God's mercies" (Rom. 12:1). This actually refers to the whole economy of grace as purchased on Calvary. A secondary or tertiary motive will not do in this situation. We must go back to the primary motive in what God does for us at Calvary through His reconciling Son.

This is typical of Paul's spiritual appeals when the issues are serious. For instance, he exhorted the church at Philippi to renounce factional motives and vanity by appealing to them to adopt the mind of Christ as portrayed in His matchless self-emptying. Your attitude must be that of Christ:

Though he was in the form of God,
he did not deem equality with God
something to be grasped at.

Rather, he emptied himself
and took the form of a slave,
being born in the likeness of men.

He was known to be of human estate
and it was thus that he humbled himself,
obediently accepting even death,
death on a Cross!   (Phil. 2:5-8)

Similarly, in writing to the church at Corinth, he exhorted them to take an offering for a specific need. He first appealed on the basis of what the churches in Macedonia had already given, despite their poverty. He also appealed to the Corinthians' record in other Christian graces previously demonstrated. But this appeal and unanswerable argument are: "You are well acquainted with the favor shown you by our Lord Jesus Christ; how for your sake he made himself poor though he was rich so that you might become rich by his poverty" (2 Cor. 8:9). Paul's

Yielding to the Spirit

appeal is: *Our small gifts cannot be denied because of God's great Gift.*

The call to supreme commitment demands this supreme motivation. Nothing else is adequate for the depths to which we must go, for this consecration involves separation and nonconformity to the world. "Do not conform yourselves to this age but be transformed by the renewal of your mind, so that you may judge what is God's will, what is good, pleasing and perfect" (Rom. 12:2). Nothing short of this bottomless commitment is an adequate expression of our love. "Your love must be sincere. Detest what is evil. Cling to what is good" (Rom. 12:9). Such a commitment is required if we are to face up to the implications of true worship—"your spiritual worship" (Rom. 12:1).

The call to present our bodies is not a physical thing only. A part is here named for the whole. It means our total man. An illustration of this principle would be when a young man proposes to his chosen one and asks her hand. He does not mean a disjoined hand; he means her entire life and affections.

Why is yielding of the will central in consecration? The real battleground of the Christian in making a complete consecration to God is born of the fact that the carnal mind is not in harmony with such a venture. The carnal mind does not yield without a struggle to the soul making a consecration that is limitless, bottomless, timeless, and without mental reservation. True consecration, however, is more than an act of the will; it involves the whole man.

Consecration, in many respects, is a demonstration of our obedience to God, and to fail to face up to its implications will place the Christian in spiritual shadows and then in darkness. God has a way of putting us to the test. Perhaps no two people ever come over identical paths to full possession of the Pentecostal blessing, although the basic issues in each case are similar.

For consecration must be real to be effective. It must be more than mental; it must be actual. It must be something far-reaching for us in order to be significant to God. To be valid as a condition, consecration must be complete—without hesitation and without reservation. Someone has truly said that the most difficult part of living the Christian life is trying to just half live it. Christian living at its best is dependent upon total surrender!

Christians do not have to struggle to receive the Holy Spirit—He is already with them. *What they must do is surrender themselves totally to the Holy Spirit who comes to indwell believers.*

There are two major fallacies concerning the Spirit-filled life. One is the concept that Spirit-filling is the result of spiritual growth and, therefore, a gradual process. Though there are many steps preparing us for the filling of the Holy Spirit, we do not grow or slide into the experience of the baptism with the Spirit.

There comes a time in our Christian lives when we realize our inner need for a deeper work of the Spirit, we make a full surrender of ourselves, and trust God to fill us with the Holy Spirit. This is as definite a crisis as conversion or the new birth.

On the other hand, it is just as wrong to look upon the fullness of the Spirit as only a crisis, resulting in a one-step, instant, and final condition of spirituality with no room for growth. *The Spirit-filled life is both a crisis and a process!*

The Christian life is dynamic and progressive. We maintain the fullness by never settling down in a static level of holiness, but by continuously receiving His infilling. Self-surrender, therefore, is both a crisis and a continuing process. There comes a moment when we surrender completely for the first time in our lives, but then the act of surrender must be followed by a day-by-day attitude of surrender and obedience.

It has been helpful for me to realize that just because I am fully surrendered to God at the moment does not mean there will never be new areas for surrender as I walk with God. In fact, daily is how often I find little and big areas of myself that need to be surrendered right there and then.

This thought illustrates the point beautifully: The light that the Holy Spirit shines into our hearts is not so much like a searchlight, suddenly turned on full power, revealing every single item in our lives that is contrary to His will. That would probably overpower and frighten us to death. The Spirit works more like a rheostat, turning up the light gradually. As it becomes

Yielding to the Spirit

brighter and brighter it exposes new area that need to be adjusted to His will. Since we have already said the big "yes" at the time of surrender, we now immediately and willingly follow with another "Yes, Lord, I surrender this too." In gratitude we say, "Lord, I didn't realize this defect in my life. Thank you for showing it to me, I am ready to obey."

When talking of surrender we are really talking about committing our wills to Jesus Christ. Psychologically speaking, we are unable to surrender anything concrete until we are aware of it.

So, in our surrender to God, we affirm our willingness to decide in God's favor whenever we are aware of a specific issue before us.

Essential to this kind of surrender is trust. It is impossible to surrender completely to God without trusting Him totally.

God says to us, "Trust Me. Believe that I have your best interest at heart and I will never leave you or forsake you. I will direct your paths if you will acknowledge Me and trust Me."

Let there be no misunderstanding. It is impossible to surrender if you do not trust!

Trust God with your life—surrender to Him your future, your everything. He is the most loving, reliable, honest, and trustworthy element in all creation. Truly blessed is the man who will say, "Lord, I renounce the right to make my choices on the basis of my own plans and desires. In every event I will always seek to know and do Your will."

We see, then, that consecration is a prerequisite to the Spirit-filled life. One must be fully surrendered and abandoned to the will of God to receive the Holy Spirit in His blessed fullness. An absolutely unconditional requirement is personal surrender, the full and trusting gift of self to the Lord of truth and wisdom.

One Spiritual writer emphasizes the value of this gift in order to achieve union with God thus: "Being unable to make a full surrender of ourselves, we are never given a fully supply of the treasure. When the self-like expires, the fullness of the Spirit comes in as naturally as air rushes into a vacuum." This abandonment has been termed in classical doctrine as "consecration," "commitment," or "death of self." But, whatever our terminology, we must come to the crisis of self-abandonment to the will of God.

Consecration moves on a deeper level than the initial surrender to Christ for pardon. Its motivation is a deepened conviction of the pervasive nature of self-will. It is the frank and contrite acknowledgment of one's pettiness, ambition, pride, and selfishness, and a conscious willing commitment of the self in love to God. Such consecration is not simply a general prayer, but a heart plea that will not be hushed until the inner self can wholeheartedly respond to the faintest whisper of God. This "death of self" is the gateway to the Spirit-filled life.

Whenever or wherever a Child of God comes to this place of self-realization of his deep need and surrenders himself fully to Christ, calling out for all of God's love, he will receive the baptism with the Spirit—no matter whether it is called "union with God," "Spirit-filled," "Infused Contemplation," "the Pentecostal Blessing," or some other terminology. When Christ answers our pleading, what else can He give? The Holy Spirit was His parting gift to His children! *Consecration + receptive faith = the mighty baptism with the Spirit!*

DEARTH OF PRAISE

Somewhere within the silent tomb of self,
Resides an unsung song of muted praise.
Long held suppressed, and placed on shrouded shelf,
Creation's gift that all God's sons might raise
Their voices to Creator, Lord and King,
So that His praise resound throughout the earth...
But captive hearts, no gifts of homage bring,
And oh, the vast wasteland that knows such dearth
Of praise because our hearts are filled with fear—
Fear of what someone may say—Pride has ways
To hold in bondage all the voiceless years,
Yet He desires that praise should fill our days.

    O Mighty God, we lift our voice to Thee:
    Cast out all self; set captive spirits free!

—*Verla A. Mooth*

4

The Purifying Flame

The baptism with the Holy Spirit in sanctifying grace is like fire. As we observe the simple operation and function of fire, in a limited sense we can understand the operation and function of the Holy Spirit in sanctifying and keeping power in the heart.

Fire has ever been the symbol of deity. God's Presence was symbolized by the flaming sword placed at the east entrance of the Garden of Eden. God revealed himself to Moses in the burning bush, which was not consumed. He was manifested to the children of Israel in the pillar of fire by night. When Elijah staged the test of deities on Mount Carmel, God displayed His power and glory with a Niagara "wall of fire" to protect His people, and He has prophesied that in the last days He will avenge the righteous by fire. He dispenses the fire that refines, the fire that empowers, the fire that destroys. Down through history the Lord has used fire as a symbol of His presence whether in wrath or mercy.

In both the Old and New Testament the Holy Spirit was described as "like the refiner's fire that burns away the dross" (Mal. 3:2-3; Matt. 3:11).

In Hebrews 12:29 we read: "For our God is a consuming fire." Fire was recognized as identical with life, and the Parsis of India today worship it with holy veneration. God has always recognized it in His Word, not as an object of superstitious regard, but as the symbol of His own transcendent glory, and the power of His presence and His Holy Spirit.

Let us look but briefly at some of the illustrations of the figure of fire in the Scripture, especially the use of fire in the Mosaic ritual. In all the sacrifices and offering fire was an important element, just as blood was. The paschal lamb was roasted in the fire and eaten by the people as a symbol of Christ's flesh prepared for us and ministered to us by the Holy Spirit as our Living Bread.

The burnt offering was consumed upon the altar by fire, the type of Christ, offered for our sins, but for our acceptance with God, and the type of our true consecration as we yield ourselves up to God by the Holy Spirit.

There are countless symbols of Christ's priesthood and also our true ministry of prayer that comes from the burning incense. But most of all, the fire that consumed the incense is the type of the Holy Spirit, without whom all our prayers and sacrifice must stop short of heaven.

No more graphic symbol can be found than that of the red heifer. This type was especially for God's people in the wilderness life. The red heifer represented Christ, our Sacrifice, slain and consumed for us on the altar of God. But in the burning of the heifer there come the scarlet wool, the cedar, and the hyssop leaves, representing something that is to be consumed along with the death of Christ.

The scarlet wool represents our sins, the cedar our strength, and the hyssop our weakness and the clinging elements in our nature.

All these things are to be crucified with Christ, and this can be done only through the power of the Holy Spirit. We are not equal to the task of self-crucifixion, but we can hand over everything and anything to Him, and consent that it shall die. Then by the power of His Holy Spirit He will put it to death and make the crucifixion real.

Even after the death of the heifer the fire was to be preserved and made perpetual by the preservation of the ashes. We know ashes are a kind of preserved fire. By pouring water upon these ashes you create lye, a very acrid, pungent, burning substance. Now, these ashes were preserved and water poured upon them, and used as a water of separation or purification when anyone had contracted any sin or defilement whatsoever.

It was the type of the work of the Holy Spirit in *constantly cleansing* us from defilement or pollution contracted from earthly things and absorbed from the atmosphere in which we live.

The Purifying Flame

This cleansing is not always pleasant. It is sometimes like the touch of lye, a consumming fire; but it is a wholesome thing, like the burning way of proud flesh by caustic, to have our very nature purified for us from self and sin.

There are so many lessons that we may learn from the figure of fire itself, but we can touch but briefly upon them. Fire is a cleansing element. It differs from water in this, that, while water cleanses externally, fire purifies internally and intrinsically, penetrating to the very substance of things, and filling every fiber and particle of matter with its own element.

Chemists tell us that fire contains three component parts: the calorific ray, the actinic ray, and the luminous energy.

The calorific ray is that property of fire that produces heat. In the physical world there would be no life without the calorific rays that come to us from the sun. This warmth God bestows upon a cold, dark, frigid world. Malachi the prophet, sensing this great truth, said in regard to Christ's coming, "But for you who fear my name, there will arise the sun of Justice with its healing rays" (Mal. 3:20).

Christ brought the warmth of God's love to man. Jesus emphasized that God is a God of love and warmth. In Christ we see the true picture of the fire of God's love and Grace. After the resurrection of Jesus, those two disciples who walked with him on the Emmaus road said, "Were not our hearts burning inside us as he talked to us on the road and explained the Scriptures to us?" (Luke 23:32).

The "fire of God," kindled in heaven, was bringing its warmth directly to man, and was producing spiritual heat through the Sun of justice who had arisen with healing rays. Sin is cold, calculating, ruthless; but justice, obtained through Christ, is warm, understanding, and compassionate.

The actinic ray is that property of fire that works chemical change. It turns wood to ashes, tempers steel, and changes the color and form of objects that come in contact with it.

It is this property in the rays of the sun that transforms seeds into plants, buds into flowers, and grass into hay. It is the miracle ray that makes useless things useful.

Like the calorific ray, it is a physical symbol of God's ability to do mightier things in the spiritual realm. When a man comes in contact with God, he can never be the same again. This "fire" either draws or drives away, saves or destroys, helps or hinders. Accepted and utilized, it becomes a boon and a blessing. Rejected, it becomes a bane and a curse. One dying thief was drawn to the warmth of the Saviour; he responded and was saved. The other dying thief turned away, rejected God's compassion; he was lost.

God takes the weak and makes them strong. He takes the vile and makes them clean. He takes the worthless and makes them worthwhile. He takes the sinful and makes them sinless.

With this in mind, Ezekiel said, "I will give you a new heart and place a new Spirit within you, taking from your bodies your strong hearts and giving you natural hearts" (Ezek. 36:26).

Fire penetrates impenetrable metal. The Holy Spirit penetrates or illuminates the heart, revealing the depths and degradation of sin and at the same time illuminating and revealing the redemptive and cleansing merits of Christ's atoning blood.

Fire is also a great cleansing or purifying agent. Laboratory technicians point out that fire is the only purifying agent found that will cleanse an object without taking on any of the characteristics of the object cleansed. The Holy Spirit is the great Cleanser or Purifier of the heart. Every person who has struggled with the impurities of his heart realizes that the purifying of the heart requires the mighty work of God.

John the Baptist does not minimize his message of repentance and baptism in water but declares that Jesus, who is greater and follows him, will provide His baptism, which is the baptism with the Holy Spirit. He praises Jesus for His baptism, which is like a mighty, cleansing, consuming, energizing fire in the soul!

It does no justice to the Spirit of God to suppose that He will baptize or fill unclean vessels. One of His great purposes in the lives of God's people was forever stated by St. Peter: "But purified their hearts by means of faith also" (Acts 15:9). Simon Peter concluded his dramatic defense of preaching to the Gen-

The Purifying Flame

tiles by stating that God gave them "the Holy Spirit just as he did to us. He made no distinction between them and us, but purified their hearts by means of faith also" (Acts 15:8-9).

The baptism of John represented the cleansing of our life and conduct, the reformation of our character, and the work of the law and the truth upon human hearts. But Christ's baptism was by fire, and went to the roots of conduct. The purity He required included motives, aims, and "the thought and intents of the heart." He not only requires but He gives the purity that springs from the depths of our being. Like the flame that consumes the dross and leaves the molten metal pure and unalloyed, so the Holy Spirit separated us from our old sinful self-life and burns into us the nature and the life of Christ.

This does not mean freedom from tests and temptations, from weakness and the possibility of failure, as erroneously thought by some of our well-meaning brothers and sisters in Christ. It means that we are to become "partakers of the divine nature" (cf. 2 Peter 1:4), as tiny rays of sunlight are partakers of the fire of the sun in the heavens and as little grains of sand are partakers of the substance of the entire earth. And the ray from the Holy Spirit quickens and gives life as it warms the soul. We are born again by the Spirit, nursed into spiritual being, and cherished into growth and maturity by the Spirit of God who is like to Fire and Flame!

The sharing of a personal experience is, in no way, an attempt to make a doctrine of it. If, however, it may be some small source of inspiration to others, it is here given: As a young girl of twelve years of age, I went to the altar in a small country church to seek the baptism with the Spirit. A child's heart is so tender—so surrendered—that it did not take long for the Fire from heaven to fall upon me. This was more than forty years ago, and, at that period, I had never seen a searchlight, for we did not even have rural electrification in our small farm community. And I am sure that it was not a matter of prior suggestion. I only know that I was *bathed* in a bright, searching light until I could actually feel the hot rays of heat upon my head. I lifted my arms to heaven and started to praise the Lord with tears of joy streaming down my face. This was the Charismatic gift of holy tears that the Spirit has flooded my soul with countless times over as He fills me with the unspeakable joy of His Presence.

During the intervening years, there have been times when I grew worldweary and skeptical of many things. But there is one thing I could never doubt: *The Precious Holy Spirit comes in Fire and and Flame to baptize His own! Praise His precious name!*

There are two special promises in the prophetic book of Malachi. The first is the coming of John the Baptist: "Behold, I will send my messenger, who shall prepare the way for me." The second is the coming of the Lord Himself in His first advent.

> And suddenly there will come to the temple
> the Lord whom you seek,
> and the messenger of the Convenant whom
> you desire,
> yes, he is coming, says the Lord of hosts.
> (Mal. 3:1)

This, of course, has reference to the coming of the Lord Jesus Christ in His incarnation and earthly ministry. But the promise immediately unfolds into a fullness of meaning that takes in also the ministry of the Holy Spirit. Indeed, the ministry of Christ and the Holy Spirit are here so linked together that it is impossible to tell where one begins and the other ends.

> But who will endure the day of his coming?
> And who can stand when he appears?
> For he is like the refiner's fire,
> or like the fuller's lye
>
> He will sit refining and purifying (silver),
> and he will purify the sons of Levi,
> refining them like gold or like silver
> that they may offer due sacrifice to the Lord.
> (Mal. 3:2-3)

The Purifying Flame

Then, later, there comes a third promise, of the day that is coming, the other fire that is to consume and burn to ashes all the dross that the fire of the Holy Spirit has not burned away. This, of course, is the day of the Lord's second coming.

But it is especially to the second of these promises that our subject holds us, the promise and the purifying fire of the Holy Spirit.

As we have seen, this work is connected directly with the personal ministry of the Lord Jesus Himself. It is spoken of as if it were all Christ's own work. But we know who it was that brought the refiner's fire and fuller's soap, the Holy Spirit. Yet it is Christ who "baptizes with the Holy Spirit," and when He comes it is Christ He brings, so that it is the one life, the one work, through the two persons of the one God.

The work He comes to do is to cleanse and purify. He is the Spirit of holiness. But, as we have seen, there are two stages of holiness suggested. The first is cleansing from sin; the second is refining the gold and bringing it to a higher measure of purity and beauty. The Spirit comes to do both these works in the believer's heart.

It is one thing to be cleansed from all known sin, but it is quite another to be refined, polished, and transformed into all the fullness of all the good and acceptable and perfect will of God. There is a good, but there is also an acceptable; and then there is the perfect will of God, and the Spirit is longing to bring us up to the highest. The wedding robe of the Bride of the Lamb is represented as not only clean, but bright; that is, glorious and beautiful, like Christ's own transfiguration robes. Iron can be refined until it is more precious than gold. So our hearts can be not only purified but glorified, even here!

Corresponding to this double work is the double figure, the refiner's fire and the fuller's soap. The soap is for outward cleansing, the fire is for inward and intrinsic transformation. Fire can penetrate where water cannot reach, and can be used where water and soap are of no avail. Fire can be used to cleanse only that which in its nature is indestructible. The silver and gold can stand the fire, because they are incombustible. The more you burn them, the more you improve them. So the fire of the Holy Spirit can come to us only when we become united with God, and partakers of His divine nature. Then we do not fear the fire. It cannot hurt us, but only refines.

Another glorious promise is found in the words "He shall sit." The Holy Spirit does not hurry the work begun in us at the time of regeneration, that is, the work of fire. He awaits our acceptance of—and longing for—the mighty baptism with the Holy Spirit, which is a deeper, intense inworking of the Holy Spirit. The figure of the Holy Spirit working as a refiner and purifier of silver suggests the thoughtful care given to the soul. He sits down in the crucible. He does not for a moment leave His precious work. He does not let the fire get too hot, or burn too long. And the moment He can see His face on the molten gold, He knows the work is complete, and the fire is withdrawn. This is the more gradual and subsequent work of our Sanctifier and Keeper in developing and filling our spiritual capacity, searching and enlarging us, and leading us on and out and up into all the fullness of the mature manhood of Christ.

Finally, all this is for service. "He will purify the sons of Levi, that they may offer unto him an offering in righteousness." This is God's great end in all His work of grace. He will not give us the Holy Spirit to terminate upon ourselves, and if He sees that our object in seeking even spiritual blessing and power is our own delight, aggrandizement, or self-importance, we shall be disappointed. But if our purpose is to be like God Himself, channels of blessings to others, and instruments for His use, He will fill us and use us to the fullest measure. *Indeed, God purifies us from our selfishness that His love might move us to compassion.* For our sakes Christ dedicated himself to Calvary—that we might find our cross and give ourselves without measure for the salvation of the world.

The baptism with the Holy Spirit is thus God's means of purifying and empowering the Church to carry forward the ministry begun by the Son. "You will receive power when the Holy Spirit comes down on you; then you are to be my witnesses in Jerusalem,

The Purifying Flame

throughout Judea and Samaria, yes, even to the ends of the earth" (Acts 1:8).

And this brings us to the third property of fire, which is luminous energy—that part of fire that is light. The Scripture points out a parallel: "God is light and in him there is no darkness" (1 John 1:5). It is the presence of God's Holy Spirit in our lives that produces divine light and spiritual illumination. When the disciples were "baptized with fire" on the day of Pentecost, their intellects were sharpened, their undrstanding was quickened, and their powers of comprehension were transformed. Who would have guessed that in that crowd of fishermen, taxgatherers, and nondescript persons were men who through the experience of that Upper Room would change the course of history?

We know that the "light" the Apostles had was not their own, but that they came into possession of it through a miracle of God when they were filled with the Holy Spirit. The luminescence of soul and mind that they owned was certainly not acquired—it was imparted. The disciples preached and wrote Godimparted truths. A Christian has never really witnessed until his witnessing is fired with the inspiration of revelation through the gifts of the Holy Spirit.

Far too many contemporary Christians seem to think that the First Pentecost was a time of glory and splendor, if not, indeed, rather calm and placid. In so doing, they fail to realize that through wind and flame men were moved from the false security of the Upper Room, and with a courage not their own were carried into a world to speak of a Man and a message that would bring the Apostles into direct confrontation with the established religion of Israel, and ultimately into confrontation with the dominant movement of Hellenic thought. And the end was a confrontation that brought martyrdom.

In this light, perhaps, we might consider revising some of our traditional Pentecostal hymns: "Come Holy Ghost, Creator Blest, and in our hearts take up thy rest." But the Holy Spirit does not really rest within our hearts. If the First Pentecost is any indication, when we open ourselves to the Spirit, we invite fire and wind. When we open ourselves to the Spirit, we make an act of deep personal surrender to an invading God—a God who imposes demands and forces us to ask questions, the kind of questions that a lost and dying world is seeking the answers for!

How can we claim to know the fullness of the Spirit if we are selfish and passionless? Only the passionate heart is pure. Only when the flames of love reach outward and upward toward others can the heart of man truly be aflame with the Fire of the Spirit.

But when the Spirit and fire of God reach down and touch the soul of finite man, gladness and assurance radiate a true spiritual likeness in him unto the Crucified Saviour who has redeemed us through His most precious blood!

5

The Person of the Spirit

We cannot rightly understand the work of the Holy Spirit or come into right relationship with the Holy Spirit himself, and thus know His gracious work in our souls, unless we acknowledge and have reverence for His true personality.

It is important that we especially emphasize the personality of the Holy Spirit.

In the full Christian revelation of God, the Holy Spirit is disclosed as genuinely personal. To speak of the Holy Spirit as *it*—as an impersonal influence or power from God—is to discredit, or at least to disregard, the clear teaching of the New Testament.

To think of the Holy Spirit as simply a power from God is to fall into a form of idolatry; it is to ask, "How can I get the Holy Spirit and use it?" God would thus be a power to be selfishly manipulated. If I think of the Holy Spirit as an impersonal force, I will ask, "How can I have more power?" But if I acknowledge Him as a Person, my concern will be "How can the Holy Spirit get more of me?" Bible religion is God-centered. Such God-centeredness is guarded by faith in the Holy Spirit as the Third Person of the Holy Trinity.

To think of the Holy Spirit as an impersonal influence is to rob Him of the worship and reverence that is due Him as the Third Person of the adorable Trinity. When Moses heard the voice of God in the burning bush, he was admonished to remove his shoes, for he was on holy ground. And we, too, would do well to remember that being in the Presence of the Lord is to be on "holy ground"! I fear that sometimes our expressions of joy may give way to childish exuberance, and exuberance give way to a type of hilarity that is not a part of the deep reverence due the Third Person of the Blessed Trinity in our worship. We are like a group of undisciplined children who run the risk of becoming excitable and overwrought in our play. As children of God, we are not only supposed to play at God's feet, *but to rest at His feet, as well.*

Some of the things that pass for "worship in the Spirit" are not only poor practices of worship—*they are in poor taste.* While it is true that there must always be room for freedom of the Spirit in our worship, there is also need for a disciplining of our spirit! To know and worship the Holy Spirit, however, is more than a matter of correct theology or behavioral patterns of worship. He must come in His personal indwelling if we are to have an *inner* and *sanctifying* knowledge of Him.

Let us consider the personality of the Holy Spirit. When we speak of the Holy Spirit as a person we do not mean that He is a bodily creature. Human persons as we know them in this life have bodies, but a body is only a means for expressing true personality. A person thinks, feels, acts. A person also makes moral choices.

Personal qualities belonging to the Holy Spirit are:

1. *Intelligence.* When we affirm that the Spirit is intelligent, then we are affirming His personality. The prophet Isaiah asks, "Who has directed the Spirit of the Lord or has instructed him as his counselor? When did he consult to gain knowledge? Who taught him the path of judgment, or showed him the way of understanding?" (Isa. 40:13-14). The same truth meets us in the New Testament "Who, for example, knows a man's innermost self but the man's own spirit within him? Similarly no one knows what lies at the depths of God but the Spirit of God" (1 Cor. 2:11,16). In Romans 8:26-27 Paul speaks of the mind of the Spirit, suggesting that there is a meaning in our prayer beyond that of which we are aware. The true intent of real prayer is the result of the work of the Holy Spirit, who guides us as we pray.

2. *Feeling.* The holy Spirit has personal feelings and emotions. In Romans 15:30 we read: "I beg you, brothers, for the sake of Our Lord Jesus Christ and the love of the Spirit; join me in the struggle by your prayers to God on my behalf." In Ephesians 4:30 we are warned. "Do nothing to sadden the Holy Spirit." The

Holy Spirit within creates divine love in our hearts, but if we give way to an un-Christlike spirit He is grieved. To persist in a wrong attitude is to grieve Him away and break His seal.

In speaking of our relationship and approach to the Holy Spirit, Rev. A. B. Simpson gives us this beautiful thought: "The Holy Ghost is very sensitive, as love always is. You can conquer a wild beast by blows and chains, but you cannot conquer a woman's heart that way, or win the love of a sensitive nature. That must be wooed by the delicate touches of trust and affection. So the Holy Ghost has to be taken by faith as delicate and sensitive as the gentle heart with whom it is coming in touch. One thought of unbelief, one expression of impatient distrust or fear, will instantly check the perfect freedom of His operations as much as a breath of frost would wither the petals of the most sensitive rose or lily. Speak to the Rock (the Living Waters), do not strike it. Believe in the Holy Ghost and treat Him with the tenderest confidence and most unwavering trust, and He will meet you with instant response and equal confidence."

These beautiful insights show us that there is no place for—or need of—prolonged agonizing, loud supplications, and excessive pleadings. "*The Rock need not be struck again, because it was already smitten and opened, and the waters are already flowing freely.*"

3. *Decision and Purpose.* In Corinthians, Paul discusses spiritual gifts. They are varied, he says, to serve different functions within the body of Christ. "But it is one and the same Spirit who produces all these gifts; distributing them to each as he wills" (1 Cor. 12:11). A person's gift is not according to his own will or choice but according to the choice of the Spirit. Although God probably takes into account our natural abilities, in the final analysis the Spirit's gifts are supernatural bestowals according to the Spirit's will.

Here we confront the matter of the call of the Spirit. I may prefer to follow a certain line of work, but I feel inwardly impelled to another type of service. The call of the old prophets and the call today to the various ministries are evidence of the planning of the Spirit. The Spirit is not a divine power we use according to our will, and our desires for ministry; *He is a Divine Person who wants to use us according to His will!*

4. *Moral Choices.* The title "Holy" applied to the Spirit of God indicates that He is a moral personality. Holiness in the moral sense can apply only to a personal being. The same conclusion concerning His moral nature is implied by the fact that He is a member of the Trinity. He who is called the Spirit of God and the Spirit of Christ must be the Holy Spirit. In the awesome warning Jesus gave to the Pharisees against blaspheming the Spirit, their danger was the danger of disregarding or defying the ultimate moral power of the universe, or doing this in such a way as to destroy all power of moral discrimination in themselves. Moreover, when the Spirit convicts us, He convicts of sin and of righteousness, and when He enters our heart in regenerating and sanctifying power He transforms us morally. *It is because He is a moral person that he is grieved by sin.*

Personal acts belonging to the Holy Spirit bear this out. Even a casual reading of the New Testament convinces us that the Spirit *acts* as a Person. Jesus promised His disciples that the Spirit would *teach* them all things and *bring* to *remembrance* all that He had said unto them while with them in the flesh (John 14:26). Notice the verbs in this passage:

> When he comes, however,
> being the Spirit of truth
> he will *guide* you to all truths,
> he will not *speak* of his own,
> but will *speak* only what he *hears*,
> and will *announce* to you the things to come.
>
> In doing this he will *give glory to me,*
> because he will have received from me
> what he will announce to you.
> (John 16:13-14)

In Acts the Spirit is said to speak, to send, to forbid, and to counsel.

The Person of the Spirit

The Spirit is associated with the Father and the Son in the work of redemption. The New Testament parallels the Holy Spirit with the other Persons of the Godhead. The Great Commission commands us:

Baptize them in the Name
of the Father
and of the Son,
and of the Holy Spirit.
(Matt. 28:19)

Paul's moving benediction in 2 Corinthians reads, "The grace of the Lord Jesus Christ, and the love of God, and the fellowship of the Holy Spirit be with you all!" (13:13).

The New Testament equates the Spirit with God. After accusing Ananias of lying to the Holy Spirit, Peter charged, "You have not lied unto men, but unto God." If the Spirit is God, and God is personal then the Spirit is personal.

Our consideration of the personality of the Holy Spirit has introduced us to the doctrine of the Trinity. Intelligent, effective Christians must have some understanding of this admittedly difficult doctrine. We cannot expect fully to comprehend the mystery of the Infinite. If we could, God would not be God. Mystery should inspire awe, worship, adoration. But mystery must not involve us in contradiction. The doctrine of the Trinity may be *beyond* reason; it must not be so stated as to be unreasonable.

The ultimate principle of the universe is One. This is so evident to reason that the old philosophers of Greece came to believe in one God apart from the special revelation to the Bible.

And here we come to the mystery of the Trinity: There are three Persons in the One God. The Bible teaches—by clear intimation in the Old Testament and by explicit statement in the New Testament—that the unity of God is not a rigid, mathematical unity. It is a rich complexity.

God is one; God is three. But God is not three in the same way that He is one—that would be nonsense. *He is one Divine*

Being within whom there are three centers of personal consciousness. The early Church said that God is one substance, within which there are three Persons. But the word *substance* suggests material stuff to the average person—and God is Spirit. *Being* is a better word than *substance*. Though we cannot comprehend God, this much we know: He is not *solitary*, He is *Social*.

The New Testament clearly teaches that the Father is God, the Son is God, the Holy Spirit is God, and, further, that wherever we meet one Person of the Godhead we meet God. The Father is God, Christ is God, the Spirit is God.

Dr. Samuel Chadwich observes: "As it pleased God that in His Son should dwell the fullness of the Godhead bodily, so it has pleased Him that in the dispensation of the Spirit there should dwell in Him the same fullness; and as in the Son the Father and the Spirit were revealed, so in the Spirit are the Son and the Father made known in the soul." As Jesus was Immanuel, God *with* us, the Holy Spirit is God *in* us.

Whatever God does, the entire Trinity does. The Three Persons are one in being, in purpose, in activity. In Christian experience we know that we have to do, not with three Gods, but with the one true and living God. Yet we participate in the One God through the special work of the Three. *Through* Christ we have access *in* the Holy Spirit *to* the Father (Eph. 2:18). To be Christian is to experience the Three-One God.

In thinking of the Trinity we must avoid the error that there are three beings—three individuals in the human sense—in the Godhead. This is the error of tritheism (three Gods) and is dangerously close to polytheism (many Gods).

Personality has two aspects—the individual and the social. The *individual* aspect is that which sets one off as distinct from every other self. The *social* aspect is that which makes us a part of everyone else and prompts us to give ourselves to others in the fellowship of love.

Applying this to the "Persons" of the Godhead, we would say that each is distinct in one sense from the other but each Person lives in and for the others. The three Persons of the God-

The Person of the Spirit

head are distinct but not separate. Each is in all, and all are in each. Thus God is not solitary but social in His being. The one God, who is holy love, is the perfect pattern of all fellowship in love.

The perplexity arises from our imperfect conception of the Persons of the Trinity. With us personality is divisive and exclusive. Each is separate from the rest and must always be a separate personality. Personality in the Trinity is not exclusive but inclusive, not divisive but inherent.

In order to appreciate the full work of the Holy Spirit, however, we need to understand the roles of Christ and of the Spirit. Philip voiced the deep yearning of the human heart when he asked the Saviour, "Shew us the Father." What is God like? What is He in His inmost heart?

The Old Testament gives us a gradual unfolding of God's self-disclosure. But God could not fully unveil himself to prophets or in parchments— *He must come to us in person.* So Jesus answered Philip, "He that hath seen me hath seen the Father." Jesus was God clothed in human personality, that we might see Him and look upon Him, and handle Him that we might *know* Him. In the words of the little child, "Jesus is the best picture God ever had took." Her grammar may have been atrocious, but her theology was apt. Since Jesus came, we know that our Father is a Christlike God.

The supreme and climatic revelation of God is the Cross and the Resurrection of Christ.

> The way we come to understand love
> was that he laid down his life for us.
> *(1 John 3:16)*

The Cross is the concrete expression of the holy love of God, which takes up into itself the suffering and alienation of sin in order to destroy it—to make atonement. The Resurrection is the assurance of the divine victory over sin, death, and hell, and the pledge to us of a living Christ.

Moreover, the Holy Spirit Came to Impart God. The Holy Spirit came to apply to our hearts the benefit of Christ's redemptive sufferings. He exists to act *within*. His it is to enter into the recesses of the human spirit and to work from within the subjectivity of man. From within our human being the Spirit vitalizes, stabilizes, renews, admonishes, warns, recalls, interprets, enlightens, guides, and gives comfort or strength. He is God in His special activity and agency of secret invasion and invisible occupation. He is the *sanctifying* Spirit—making us holy even as the Father is holy.

If God's self-revelation climaxed in Jesus' life, death, and resurrection, His self-impartation climaxed in His coming through the Spirit at Pentecost to indwell and sanctify His people. Jesus is God *with* us; the Holy Spirit is God *in* us.

Perhaps the most familiar concept of the Holy Spirit held by many Christians is that of the Holy Spirit as *the Comforter*. The Greek word *paraclete* so translated means "one called to stand beside us." The exact English equivalent is the word *advocate*. The Holy Spirit, Jesus promised, shall be with us—in us—to counsel us, to guide us, to help us, to console us in the dark night of suffering and sorrow.

The English word *Comforter* comes from two words meaning "with strength." The Holy Spirit is our divine Strengthener and Helper. He is with us to give wisdom, encouragement, and inspiration. And in the night of desolation He will cheer us with His warmth and love.

For the distinctive teaching of the New Testament is that the Spirit of God is the Spirit of Christ. He is the Spirit of Christ because Christ was the Bearer and Baptizer with the Spirit. In the Book of Acts and in the Epistles of the New Testament the Spirit is called the Spirit of Jesus, the Spirit of Christ, the Spirit of Jesus Christ, and the Spirit of the Lord (or the Lord the Spirit).

Let us look at the truth that the Holy Spirit is "Christ's other Self." To the disciples who were despondent at the thought of Jesus' departure from them the Saviour promised,

The Person of the Spirit

> I will ask the Father
> and he will gives you another Paraclete
> to be with you always;
>
> I will not leave you orphaned;
> I will come back to you.
> (John 14:16, 18)

All that Christ had been to His disciples the Comforter was to be—and more. As long as Jesus was with them in the flesh, the Spirit was with them in His person; but Jesus promises, "After my departure to the Father, He shall be *within* you." This is why he said,

> Yet I tell you the sober truth:
> It is much better for you that I go.
> If I fail to go,
> the Paraclete will never come to you.
> Whereas if I go,
> I will send him to you.
> (John 16:7)

In bestowing the Spirit, Christ was himself returning to dwell within their hearts. *The indwelling Spirit is the indwelling Christ.*

For this reason the New Testament speaks of the indwelling presence sometimes as the Spirit, sometimes as Christ. Paul says in one place, "Christ liveth in me." In another place he speaks just as emphatically and tells us that we are the temples of the Holy Spirit. He prays for the Ephesians that Christ may dwell in their hearts and that they might be "filled with all the fullness of God." To the same readers he says, "Be filled with the Spirit."

There is no confusion of Persons in these passages. Christ, who is "the fullness of God," inhabits the temples of our hearts through the Spirit. There are two Persons but only one experience.

This brings us to two facts:

First, the "fruits of the Spirit" describes the very essence of Christ's character—love, joy, peace, patient endurance, kindness, generosity, faith, mildness, and chastity (Gal. 5:22-23). Schleiermacher said many years ago, "The fruits of the Spirit are the virtues of Christ."

Second, everything the Bible says about the attitudes and dispositions of Jesus is true not only of the Father but also of the Spirit.

The term *spirit* also has two very clear meanings in the Bible. It means *a center of personal life considered apart from anything material.* Examples are "Holy Spirit," "Spirit of man," "Spirit of God," "the human spirit."

But *spirit* also means the whole attitude and disposition of a person. Thus we speak of "a right spirit" or say, "He has a Christlike spirit."

"The Spirit of Christ" properly means both. The phrase describes the Holy Spirit, the Third Person of the adorable Trinity. It also means the disposition and character that can only be called "Christlike."

The late E. Stanley Jones wrote: "If God is a Christlike God, then it follows that the Spirit is a Christlike Spirit. The same content of character will be in both. Then if the Spirit lives within us, He will not make us other than Christlike. . . . If we are made other than Christlike, it is some other spirit that possesses us—the spirit of weakness, of folly, of clannishness, of harshness, not the Holy Spirit. For the Spirit will not make us other than Christlike."

Of a truth, it may be said that *the Holy Spirit glorifies Christ!* There is about that Holy Spirit an incurable tendency to self-effacement. Jesus said that He would not speak of Himself, but rather, "He will give glory to me, because he will have received from me what he will announce to you." As Christ came to glorify-reveal—the Father, the Spirit came to glorify Christ, that Christ may be "all, and in all."

To hold, as some do, that in regeneration we receive Christ,

The Person of the Spirit

and that in the baptism of the Holy Spirit we receive the Holy Spirit is wrong for two reasons. First, it makes a false, unscriptural separation between Christ and the Spirit. Second, it overlooks the cardinal truth that the Holy Spirit comes to exalt and manifest Christ in our lives. *To be filled with the Spirit is not simply to enjoy some mystical or emotional experience; it is to be invaded and possessed by he Spirit of Christ.* There will be emotion, true enough, but emotion directed and controlled toward Christlikeness. The Corinthians thought that to be filled with the Spirit meant simply ecstasy; Paul informed them it meant to have divine love (1 Cor. 13:1-7). The spiritual man, he said, has "the mind of Christ" (1 Cor. 2:15-16). This is true sanctification, for it is total sanctity.

Lastly, the Spirit of God is the Spirit of Christ. To the Romans Paul wrote: "But you are not in the flesh, you are in the Spirit, since the Spirit of God dwells in you. If anyone does not have Spirit of Christ, he does not belong to Christ" (Rom. 8:9). The final proof that we know the indwelling of the Spirit is that we manifest the Spirit of Christ.

All that God does for us is to one end—that we might be able to confess with Paul: "And the life I live now is not my own; Christ is living in me. I still live my human life, but it is a life of faith in the Son of God, who loved me and gave himself for me" (Gal. 2:20).

Jesus himself is the major source of Biblical truth about the Holy Spirit. John 14:15-17;14:26;15:26;16:7-11; and 16:13-14 are the key passages. Here Jesus says that the Holy Spirit is a Comforter or Counselor just as He himself had been.

As we have noted, the Greek term translated Comforter or Counselor is *Paracletos*. It means a witness, a helper, an adviser, a lawyer, a strengthener, a person to be by one's side. There is absolutely no way it can properly be used to describe an influence or a power. The occasional use of a neuter pronoun in the Greek New Testament to agree with the neuter noun *pneuma* (spirit) does not void this truth.

In John 14:26;15:26;16:7-8 and 13, the masculine pronoun is explicitly used: "He shall teach you all things. He shall testify of me. . . . I will send him. . . . He will reprove the world. . . . When he, the Spirit of truth, is come, he will guide you. . . . He will not speak from himself, but what things he hears, he will speak" (Greek). No honest translator could render these pronouns *it*. They can refer only to a divine Person who teaches, testifies, guides, reproves, hears, and speaks.

What Jesus taught, the balance of the New Testament reinforces. In Acts 10:19-20, "The Spirit said" to Peter "Go with them." The Holy Spirit said, "Set apart Barnabas and Saul for me to do the work for which I have called them" (Acts 13:2; see also Heb. 3:7-11). No force, power or influence could speak or use the personal pronouns *I* and *Me*.

To have a right understanding of the Person of the Spirit is vital to having a right relationship with the Spirit. Even though it stems from a lack of understanding, there is much that is wanting in the way we speak about the Holy Spirit! A whole new jargon has been built up around the ministry of the Holy Spirit that not only fails to express the proper work of the Holy Spirit, but borders on disrespect.

For example: When one has been emotionally stirred by the Presence of the Holy Spirit, or has felt the Spirit's influence in a special, or powerful way, there are the terms "zapped" by the Spirit or "slain in the Spirit," which are not only grammatically incorrect but are expressive of the emotional and physical responses of the person, rather than of the action of the Holy Spirit.

There is much that comes from the excitability of the human psyche that is attributed to the Holy Spirit. This subject has been treated by some very wonderful scholars and is worthy of much more thought. May it suffice for this writer simply to say: Let us watch both our theology and our terminology in speaking of the work and ministry of the Holy Spirit and be sure that we attribute to the Spirit only actions and works that are worthy of the grandeur and nature of the Almighty God.

6

The Spirit's Fullness

Seventy-five years before the terms *charismatic* and *ecstatic* became common in religious vocabulary, Boston University's great Bible scholar Daniel Steele used them in an interesting and instructive context. Studying what the Scripture says about the fullness of the Spirit in both the Old and the New Testaments, Dr. Steele found three kinds of fullness described.

The first of these he called "charismatic." It literally means the gifts of God or the divine gifts of power and abilities surpassing the human.

"Charismatic" fullness is illustrated in the Old Testament very clearly and among the disciples of Jesus before Pentecost, as well as the many miracles they performed after Pentecost.

The Spirit of the Lord, coming upon Bezaleel, Gideon, Samson, and Saul—to name but four representative figures—enabled them to do what they could not have done in their own unaided strength.

The seventy disciples of Jesus, sent out to proclaim Christ's own soon-coming to the towns and villages of Palestine, were given power to heal the sick, to tread unharmed on serpents and scorpions, and to cast out demons (Luke 10:1-22). They were not to glory in this, however, but to rejoice that their names were written in heaven.

The second kind of fullness Dr. Steele names "ecstatic." It is the fullness of joy seen in Zacharias (Luke 1:67-69) and in Simeon (Luke 2:25-35) at the birth of John the Baptist and the dedication of Jesus in the temple.

David prayed for this in the Psalm:

A clean heart create for me, O God,
and a steadfast spirit renew within me.

> Cast me not out from your presence,
> and your holy spirit take not from me.
> (Ps. 5:12-13)

It is the third kind of fullness that is specially the heritage of God's people in this present age of the Spirit, which must imply the permanent gracious prescence in the soul of the Holy Spirit, in his fullness, not as an extraordinary gift, but as a person having the right of way through soul and body, having the keys even to the inmost rooms, illuminating every closet and pervading every crevice of the nature, filling the entire being with holy love. This we may call the "ethical fullness," or "fullness of righteousness," to distinguish it from the "ecstatic" and "charismastic fullness."

It is ethical fullness that creates Christlike purpose within and truly enables us to be "sharers of the divine nature, having fled a world corrupted by lust" (2 Peter 1:4).

Ethical fullness of the Spirit is peerless as it stands alone towering above other things of greatest worth in heaven or on earth, for time and for eternity. Ethical fullness is the righteousness of God. It is imparted to man. It is God's nature that has come to dwell in the human heart. It is God's holiness within man that makes him pure in his thoughts, his word, and his deeds. As we have seen, man is holy only as long as he is possessed by the Holy Spirit in all His fullness. The indwelling Spirit seeks only to do the will of God on earth as it is in heaven. From within come righteousness and truth. It is the culmination of all that is noble, good, true, right, and beautiful.

In an age when the spectacular is apt to be more esteemed than the fruit of the Spirit, it is good to hear again a voice from the past, and to harken to its wisdom.

For without a delicate balance of the ethical fullness along with the charismatic and ecstatic fullness of the Spirit, they may easily degenerate into a pseudo-Pentecostalism that seeks only signs and wonders. Here again we must also remember that even the gifts can be counterfeited. *The fruit must be in evidence in the life of the Spirit-filled Christian.*

The Spirit's Fullness

But there must also be a perfectly balanced blending of the charismatic and ecstatic fullness with the ethical fullness or we run the risk of a rigid, self-righteous legalism that masks as true holiness, but is lacking in both the purity and the power—the true marks of the Spirit's fullness.

Actually, both the fruit and the gifts are necessary for God's full will. *It is possible to manifest either without the other, but impossible for either to have full expression without the other!*

First, let us consider the "charismatic" fullness. As we can see from the very name "Charismatic Renewal," there is a tremendous revival of interest among Christian people in our day in the gifts of the Spirit. In as far as it is Biblical, this is all to the good. But with attention to the gifts of the Spirit there must be equal concern for the graces (fruit) of the Spirit or the result is a parody of the Christian life. The Apostle Paul gives two major lists of the gifts and graces of the Spirit. There are nine in each list. These gifts are named in 1 Corinthians 12:8-10. A very different list is given in Romans 12:6-8, in which are added "ministry" (serving), exhortation, giving, and showing mercy.

It is important to see that there is a major difference between the possession of the gifts and the possession of the fruit of the Spirit. Paul insists three times that spiritual gifts are distributed differently to different people in the Church according to the will of God and for profit or advantage to the Kingdom. There are different gifts, but the same Spirit. To each person the manifestation of the Spirit is given for common good. To one the Spirit gives wisdom in discourse, to another the power to express knowledge. Through the Spirit one receives faith; by the same Spirit another is given the gift of healing, and still another, miraculous powers. But it is one and the same Spirit who produces all these gifts, distributing them to each as He wills.

Again in a series of rhetorical questions in verses 29-30, Paul asks, "Are all apostles? are all prophets? are all teachers? Do all work miracles or have the gift of healing? Do all speak in tongues; all have the gift of interpretation of tongues?" The obvious answer in each case is "No." Some gifts are even better than others and Christians are to desire the greater gifts (verse 31).

In Romans 12:6, the Apostle says, "We have gifts that differ according to the favor bestowed on each of us," once more stressing the point that the gifts of the Spirit are different in each Christian's life.

In complete contrast to this is the fact that the list of graces is given in the singular: "The fruit of the Spirit is . . . ," not "The fruits of the Spirit are. . . ." This means that the same qualities of Christlikeness are to be found in all in whom the Spirit's fruit appears.

In fact, from what the New Testament says about God's kind of love, it may well be said that the other eight graces are really manifestations of love in the varied relationship and functions of life. God does not give love to one man, joy to another, peace to a third, patient endurance to still another. All the graces are essential to the reality of any.

The gifts, however, are like the individual members of the physical body—foot, hand, ear, nose, head. Yet, with all its variety in the use of its members, the body is one. The variety of members is intended to increase the unity of the whole.

Actually, of course, only one of the gifts caused any problem in Corinth, and this was the gift of tongues or languages (cf. 1 Cor. 14). And this still remains a problem for many well-meaning Christians today.

Obviously the first question is: What exactly is the gift of tongues as it appears in the New Testament? The chief sources are Acts 2 and 1 Corinthians 14. People have sometimes denied that both passages are really talking about the same thing: in Acts 2 it seems that the apostles are speaking languages needed to communicate with the international crowd of people assembled in Jerusalem, whereas in 1 Corinthians 14 someone speaking in tongues is "not speaking to men, but to God," his words being unintelligible to men.

But if we look more closely at Acts 2, we shall see that there too the apostles are not really speaking to men, except indirectly. They were all "filled with the Holy Spirit. They began to express themselves in foreign tongues and make bold proclamation as the Spirit prompted them" (Acts 2:4). And apparently they made

The Spirit's Fullness

such a noise that a crowd gathered, and was amazed to recognize all their different languages; but they were *overhearing* the apostles praying and praising God, "declaring the greatness of God."

The new song that God Himself puts into the mouth of His people, (Ps. 39:4), new born by the gift of His own divine life, is a song of praise. It is a song that they sing in simplicity and joy, and filled with wonder and amazement.

And it is precisely praise that the wondering crowd heard in so many different languages at Pentecost: "Yet each of us hears them speaking in his own tongue about the marvels God has accomplished" (Acts 2:11).

As little children, newly born by God's grace, it is quite right and fitting that we should offer Him our bodies in vocal prayer that makes no sense to us, praying, as St. Paul says (1 Cor. 14:14), with our "spirit" (by which the apostle means the nonrational part of us).

But we must also "pray with the mind" (1 Cor. 14:15). "This means that the man who speaks in tongues should pray for the gift of interpretation" (14:13). *St. Paul is not repudiating tongues, in which he himself rejoices; only tongues needs to mature into the companion gift of interpretation, in which the mind too is transformed and renewed, filled with a kind of intimate knowledge of God which Scripture calls "prophecy."* "1 should like it if all of you spoke in tongues, but I much prefer that you prophesy" (14:5).

Endowed, therefore, with the Holy Spirit, we should "grow in the knowledge of God" (Col. 1:10). St. Paul prays for the Ephesians that God will give them "a Spirit of wisdom and revelation" so that the eyes of their heart may be opened to spiritual vision, sensitive to God's will, supernaturally enlightened to know him (Eph. 1:17).

It is surely suggestive in this connection that St. Peter explains the outburst of speaking in tongues at Pentecost with reference to Joel 2:28: "It shall come to pass in the last days, says God, that I will pour out a portion of my spirit on all mankind; your sons and daughters shall prophesy" (Acts 2:17).

There is a manifold variety in the gifts of the Spirit. To each is given the manifestation of the Spirit for the common good. Although it is "according to each man's ability" (Matt. 25:14), these are gifts of the Spirit. God bestows in line with our natural aptitudes, however, and we have varying capabilities. To each his gift, as God wills. The baptism with the Spirit does not make everyone a flaming evangelist, teacher, healer, or minister. He gives the Spirit to some that they may be ministers of helpfulness; to some that they may be sanctified mothers and fathers who are keepers at home and miracles of patience, wisdom, and sweetness. To each there is a gift of the Spirit, and, whatever the kind of gift, there is to all the gift of power for effective service and testimony.

Regarding the gifts of the Spirit mentioned in 1 Corinthians 12, anyone who disparages a single one of the Spirit's gifts will find difficulty in receiving any of them; in fact, he is generally devoid both of the grace of the Holy Spirit and His power. On the other hand, we do not believe that any of the gifts of the Spirit are given as special evidence that one is baptized with the Spirit, but he exercises the gift *because* he is baptized with the Spirit. Actually, the Spirit's gifts are manifestations of the Holy Spirit in different ministries as the Spirit wills, and so none of these should be disparaged or called of small account. Since they are gifts of love from God, it is not proper to call any of them unimportant or little, or obsolete, even though we may call some of them the greater gifts.

Moreover, the Scripture cited above in support of the "variety of gifts" is not to be confused with the Scriptures in support of the initial evidence of the Spirit baptism, which was given at Pentecost, in the home of Cornelius, to the Ephesian disciples, and so on (cf. Acts 2:4; 8:17-18; 10:44-46; 19:6; 9:17-18; 1 Cor. 14:18).

In considering the initial evidence spoken of by the Scriptures, we may probably take into account that tongue speaking was something quite common in the religious world, even the pagan world, of the early days. No prejudices had to be removed, no fears overcome, and no doubtful questions answered.

The Spirit's Fullness

Today, however, many Christians have been frightened away from this gift by those who ascribe tongue speaking, as it occurs today, to either demonic or merely psychological and emotional influences.

The result is that even among children of God who earnestly seek the baptism with the Holy Spirit, there are many who are afraid of tongue speaking. They tend to resist any urge to let the Spirit use their tongue. It may be necessary that a deep inner healing take place before this resistance is overcome.

The Holy Spirit, of course, is fully able to overcome all these obstacles, and sometimes He does, gloriously. But He does not always do so, for reasons known to Himself.

The Holy Spirit is both gracious and wise. He does not force a particular gift upon His children until they are ready to accept it. At the same time, He does not deny or withhold His blessed fullness from them if they have met all the conditions and have hungered and thirsted after His presence! He will swiftly alight upon the life of one whose hand of faith beckons for His infilling presence.

Such was the case with the author, who had been subjected to a very frightening and almost spiritually disastrous malpractice by well-meaning Pentecostals as a young lady in my late teens. I will not go into this malpractice of urging seekers after the baptism with the Spirit to pray loud, repetitive prayers, in a deeply emotional and excitable state, except to say, "It is much easier to hinder the work of the Holy Spirit than to help in these matters."

But can we truly say that we have made a full and complete surrender to the Holy Spirit unless we have surrendered all our fears and psychological hangups? For those who may have fear in regard to any of the manifestations or gifts of the Holy Spirit as a true gift from God, let us consider the words of Jesus: "Would one of you hand his son a stone when he asks for a loaf, or a poisonous snake when he asks for a fish? If you, with all your sins, know how to give your children what is good, how much more will your heavenly Father give good things to anyone who asks him!" (Matt. 7:9-11).

In Isaiah, the twenty-eighth chapter, we read:

> Yes, with stammering lips and in a
>   strange language
> he will speak to this people
>   to whom he said:
> This is the resting place,
>   give rest to the weary;
> here is repose—
>   but they would not listen.
> *(Verses 11-12)*

This is the blessed rest which the Apostle Paul spoke of: ". . . Therefore a Sabbath rest still remains for the people of God. And he who enters into God's rest, rests from his own work as God did from his" (Heb. 4:3; 4:9-10).

For the Spirit-baptized Christian, the Pentecost event is not a past mystery to be recalled, but a present mystery ever constituting the reign of the Spirit in the heart of the faithful. "Reign" here is exactly what is meant. The Holy Spirit rules as Lord and exercises a royal imperium over the whole of one's life. All of the faculties are placed under the Spirit's control. As in the circumcision under the Old Law, the infilling Spirit has taken the tongue—the unruly member of the body—and circumcised (released) it to sing His praise for the edification of the spiritual man and the glory of God.

Even though different Christians receive different gifts from God in an intensely personal way, nevertheless all of them are intended for the good of the whole Church: "To each person the manifestation of the Spirit is given for the common good" (1 Cor. 12:7).

Now, the most basic way in which each one of us contributes to the good of the whole mystical Body of Christ, the Church, is by ourselves being healthy members of that Body. And "he who speaks in tongues builds up himself" (1 Cor. 14:4). The chief purpose of tongues is to help us become, through the working of God's grace, the kind of people who really embody the Chris-

The Spirit's Fullness

tian life, the kind of people whose light shines as unavoidably and naturally as that of a town on the top of a hill (cf. Matt. 5:14). *This is the manifestation of the Spirit!*

When God called Abraham, He said to him,

> I will make of you a great nation,
> and I will bless you;
> I will make your name great,
> so that you will be a blessing.
> (Gen. 12:2)

He does not bestow His gifts and graces upon us that we may exploit them selfishly. No, He blesses us that we might in turn be a blessing to others. Jesus says,

> I am the true Vine
> and my Father is the Vinegrower.
> He prunes away
> every barren branch
> but the fruitful ones
> he trims clean
> to increase their yield
> (John 15:1-2)

When the Holy Spirit comes in His fullness, our natural powers are vitalized, our dormant capacities are quickened, our human capabilities are reinforced. The mind receives a new alertness of understanding and keenness of insight. The heart finds a new simplicity of motive and intensity of devotion. We begin to become effective for God.

This, however, is a problem area for many sincere Spirit-filled Christians. They have preconceived ideas of how the Spirit of God will use them. They expect to be endowed with marvelous and miraculous powers for service and soul winning. They have heard how God has turned commonplace persons into marvels of power, and they look in vain for the same results in their own lives. Thus they are thrown into confusion and distress until, at times, they even begin to doubt the reality of their baptism with the Spirit. Such persons need to be reminded that there is a distinct difference between the gifts of the Spirit and the fruit of the Spirit. If gifts are for service, fruit is for character. Gifts are functional; fruit is a quality of life. The final proof that we are possessed and indwelt by the Holy Spirit is the beauty and power of Christlike love subduing and sanctifying us.

It is possible to produce all the outward signs of faith, all the outward evidence of the Holy Spirit, without the reality of faith, without the reality of the indwelling Holy Spirit. The Spirit-filled life does not consist essentially of signs and "spiritual" manifestations, even though these may be the normal expression of the presence of Christ. Tongues and other such gifts are a "manifestation of the Spirit," but they are not themselves the Spirit. The Spirit-filled life consists essentially in love, that divine love poured out in our hearts by the Holy Spirit, whose chief exemplar is the love of our Lord himself.

This love of which I speak is slow to lose patience—it looks for a way of being constructive. It is not possessive; it neither is anxious to impress nor does it cherish inflated ideas of its own importance.

Love has good manners and does not pursue selfish advantages. It is not touchy. It does not compile statistics of evil or gloat over the wickedness of other people. On the contrary, it is glad with all good men when truth prevails. Neither are there limits to love's endurance, no end to its trust, no fading to its hope; it will outlast anything. It is, in fact, the only thing that stands when all else has fallen.

Or, as St. Paul puts it in Galatians, "The fruit of the Spirit is love, joy, peace, patient endurance, generosity, mildness, chastity" (Gal. 5:22-23). Observe that the word *fruit* is singular. As we have pointed out, the number is plural but the grammar is correct—for the fruit is a manifestation of Love. Joy is love exulting in God. Peace is love resting in God. Patient endurance, kindness, and mildness are love subduing our spirits and making them like the Saviour. Faith is love clinging to God. Chastity is love controlling the entire being .

The Spirit's Fullness

As Christ came to be the perfect pattern of the Spirit-filled life, when we are filled with the Spirit our lives will flower with His gracious virtues. *The fruit of the Spirit is the virtues of Christ.* "Let this mind be in you which was also in Christ Jesus."

And this is what we mean by the "fullness of righteousness," without which the fullness of the Spirit would be lopsided and deformed. *In truth, it would not be the fullness of the Spirit at all!*

Unfortunately, there are no external criteria other than the fruit of the Spirit guaranteed to yield true discernment of the Spirit's fullness. Discernment is itself a working of "spirit" (cf. 1 Cor. 12:10), and as such it too needs discerning. It is by the Spirit that we recognize the Spirit. The key words here are "sanctity and sanity"; "holiness" and "wholeness"—they must walk hand in hand!

7

Power from on High

One of the most popular words in today's vocabulary is the word *power*. Statesmen and politicians speak often these days of the realignment of political power. Scientists speak of the power of their space vehicles. Military men speak of the power of their guns or planes or missiles.

Psychologists speak of the power released in human personality when the individual is no longer in the grip of a deep conflict or neurosis. Others speak of "black power" or "brown power" or "people power."

How refreshing it is, in a world so fascinated by and obsessed with power, and in a time when there is so much talk of "power shortages," to hear Jesus say, "You will receive power!"

But when is this power that Jesus promised to be received? At some future date? At death? After death? No, *Jesus never postpones the essential equipment for abundant and effective living for some future date!*

We may postpone accepting what He offers, but His provision for living a full and abundant life can be realized *now*, in this present world, through the power of the indwelling Holy Spirit.

Is this power of the Holy Spirit promised to everyone, indiscriminately? No. As we have already noted, the power of God's Spirit is promised only to those who have come to know Jesus Christ in personal salvation.

Sinners are promised pardon. But the promise of the power of the Holy Spirit is only to those who are already following Christ. Jesus never promised the power of the Spirit to pagans or nonbelievers. It was to His own disciples that Jesus said, "You will receive power when the Holy Spirit comes upon you."

It was to those whose names, He said, were already written in heaven that Jesus promised the power of the Holy Spirit. It

Power from on High

was for His own disciples that Jesus prayed so fervently, "Father, consecrate them."

His disciples had followed Jesus for three years, had heard His masterful messages, had witnessed His spectacular healings; but they still had something they didn't need, and they needed something they didn't have.

What they had that they didn't need was the carnal mind, the inward pollution, the sin principle that God said was enmity against Him. What they needed was an enduement of power that would make them adequate to meet the challenges and responsibilities of Christian discipleship in the days ahead.

On the Day of Pentecost, both of those needs were met; their hearts were purified, as Peter said, and they received the power of the Holy Spirit—both needs were met in the experience of the baptism with the Holy Spirit.

Jesus himself warned of the danger of a heart being emptied —and then standing vacant. Other devils could come to occupy it, Jesus said, until its corruption would be worse than before.

And when God accepts the consecration of a life when it is complete, He cleanses it; but He doesn't leave it empty—He fills what He cleanses. No life stands empty.

Those disciples met far more persecution after Pentecost than they had ever experienced before. But whereas *before* Pentecost they had failed or fled or denied their Lord, *after* Pentecost they were strong, steadfast, and courageous even in the face of death.

And multitudes since that first Christian Pentecost have met the conditions of surrender and faith, of full consecration and trust, and God the Holy Spirit has come to them in cleansing power. Through the power operating out of a clean heart, they have been enabled to live abundantly—sometimes facing incredible odds, but living "not somehow, but triumphantly."

The witness of those, from the Day of Pentecost on, who have yielded themselves completely to God has been that God not only cleansed their hearts but filled them with the power of His indwelling presence that enabled them to meet whatever they had to meet—and to meet it with victory and inner triumph.

For the benefits of Calvary have never been exhausted; the power in the Blood has never lessened or weakened; the grace of God has never lost its sufficiency. We may still be "endued with power from on high."

There is power to witness, to work, and to win. There is power for living and for liberty. There is power to stay clean in a dirty world. The power of God is not limited in degree or duration. There are no impossible cases or unconquerable crises with Him.

It has been said that man's extremity is God's opportunity. Without reservation we can say that Christ makes the difference in every crisis. He is scripturally our "wisdom, and righteousness, and sanctification, and (final) redemption." Trust in Him brings not only contentment but also power.

God's hand over ours will help us steer safely through life's shoals and reefs, which threaten spiritual shipwreck. In Him our weakness becomes strength, and our desperate trying becomes triumphant. Opportunities become successful operations, and challenges become successful conquests.

This does not rule out difficult and distressing places in Christian experience, but it ensures power to be all that God would have us be, and to do all that He would have us do. Spirit-filled personalities become power-full. The Spirit's baptism is for power-hungry people.

We must admit unhappily that Christians do act at times in sub-Christian ways. The problem is not alleviated by castigating them as backsliders. By such actions not only do we become liable as unrighteous judges, but also we may be denying a hidden grace at work within the other person. This does not miss blasphemy too far.

The Christian in the throes of spiritual conflict sometimes reveals the earthiness of his vessel. The quality needs improving, but there is no doubt about whose hands are molding it and the holy use to which those hands are putting it.

There must be no condoning of sin, no excuse for wrong action. Sin is conquered in the Christian's life. But our failures must be acknowledged, rectified, and by God's grace not repeated. Such confession and immediate divine forgiveness can keep our relationship with the Lord intact. Experiencing the power of the Spirit's purifying love will prevent us from moral defeat. The Holy Spirit will even use our predicaments, our failures, as occasions for sanctifying us at deeper levels where our spiritual awareness is sensitized and our implicit obedience is prompted by a primary love for God. This is the growth that always happens in the Spirit-filled life, because "God's love has been poured into our hearts through the Holy Spirit" (Rom. 5:5).

The Master knew that it was quite natural and necessary for man to seek modes of influence and persuasion by which to achieve social and spiritual goals for the well-being of society. His disciples, acting in His name and pursuing Kingdom ends, would need power. Thus His gift to them upon leaving this earthly sphere was *Pentecostal power!*

Varied were the effects of the Holy Spirit's descent upon the 120 in the Upper Room on the fiftieth day after the Cross and the Resurrection. The dynamic inspired by the Spirit evidenced itself in many forms.

1. There was the power of unity. They were a people of "one accord." Love implanted by the Holy Spirit welded them into a harmonious and inseparable unit. Togetherness? They really had it!

2. There was the power of spiritual illumination and understanding. The Holy Spirit shed a sharp light upon the history of God's dealings with Israel and the ministry and death of Christ. Witness the masterful, insightful message of Peter (Acts 2) and Stephen (Acts 7).

3. There was the power of peaceful hearts. Prior to Christ's ascension His followers were uncertain about "the shape of things to come" (cf. Acts 1:6). But in the Upper Room all had been resigned to God, and from there they went contentedly and committedly to their task of winning their neighbors.

4. There was the power of enthusiasm and inspiration. They were an ecstatic people, who went about their living with great excitement. Hear them say joyfully, "We can't keep quiet about our experience; it's too good!" (cf. Acts 4:20).

But Pentecost's thrust would have died shortly if its dynamic had been only a matter of unity, illumination, peacefulness, and inspiration. In the hour of test, when motives and ethics were attacked, the cause would have perished as quickly as it had been inaugurated had there not been a deeper power.

Pentecost brought into the hearts of those Upper Room supplicants the *power of purity*. Pure hearts were created there, and in that fact lies the permanence and the power of that memorable feast.

When the Holy Presence descended, He came with the power and grace to make the hearts and lives of men clean, both within and without, in action and attitude. That first Christ-centered group wanted just such power. Devoted believers want such an experience today.

For a pure heart exercises a silent, inescapable strength. Tennyson has one of his characters say:

*My strength is as the strength of ten
Because my heart is pure.*

Why is there power in purity?

1. *It creates trust.* A pure heart will show its motives in due time, and, if they are holy, they will draw others. Transparency of character bears its own store of magnetic power.

2. *It arouses thirst.* Sin's complete defeat in the heart by the work of the Holy Spirit provides the basis for freedom and a sense of security under God. The infilling of the Spirit likewise brings an adequacy of life. Here again is where purity of heart will turn a needy sinner toward spiritual things. If consistency prevails, he will submit, in time, to Christ.

3. *It releases talents.* All things being equal, a man with a pure heart will bring out the best in others. The personal resources of others can in turn be employed in the program of God.

Pentecost power is given that we might truly be witnesses to the world, to bring others to God. This is the power of powers that ultimately can destroy all other evil forces and at the same time infuse the good influence of mankind with integrity and

Power from on High

kindness. Pentecost power is the ability to influence other lives unto redemption.

The tests of being filled with the Holy Spirit are twofold, just the same today as at Pentecost. What are the tests? First, the power to live pure and holy in a sinful world. The second test is power to witness and win others to Christ.

The inherent danger here, however, is one of getting the cart before the horse. How often we are prone to expect the power to *do* to result automatically in the power to *be*. Because the power of action often brings the glory and praise we humans crave, we try to seek it apart from the inner power of holy being. This can result only in a parody of the true power of the Spirit.

We have missed the essential lesson of the New Testament if we think of the call to holiness of heart and life as just a summons to "try harder and achieve more." The men and women we meet in Acts and in the Epistles who had experienced Pentecost and were living a life of holiness are not people who were "trying harder," but are men and women *whose lives were open to the continuing penetration and power of the Holy Spirit!*

The opening of a flower occurs not because it is "trying harder"; it is the natural result of the influences of sunshine and rain. And so it is in the life of holiness: it is not by straining and struggling and feverish activity that one comes more and more to "the measure of the stature of the fullness of Christ," but by openness to the influence of God's Holy Spirit.

There is simply too much stress written on the face of too much of today's holiness. Too much strain. Too much pruning, and not enough sunshine. Too much striving to be spiritual, and not enough joyful receptivity to the influences of the Spirit, which alone can produce Christlike character.

The Apostle Paul strikes the authentic note in his letter to the Philippians. "My prayer," he says, "is that your love may more and more abound—It is my wish that you may be found rich in the harvest of justice which Jesus Christ has ripened in you, to the glory and praise of God." "It is God who, in his good will toward you, begets in you any measure of desire or achievement" (Phil. 1:9-11;2:13).

So it is not by "trying harder and doing more" that true goodness, that true holiness, that true Christlikeness is achieved, but by loving and trustful receptivity to the continuing challenges of God's purpose and power.

Of course there are demands in a life of holiness. But, as is often observed, holiness is not first a demand; it is an offer. And unless the offer is accepted, the demand cannot be met. Only an expectant openness and an eager obedience to the continuing influence and challenges of God's Spirit will produce the power that radiates out of a pure heart!

For fundamentally the power of the Holy Spirit is not to do but to be. The greatest sermons are those preached unconsciously. St. Francis of Assisi invited one of his young friars to go to the city with him to preach. After transacting some business the two started back to the countryside. The friar turned to St. Francis and said, "I thought we were going to the city to preach." "We have been preaching" was the saint's unforgettable reply.

Who can estimate the power of a holy life? Skeptics may answer many of our arguments; they cannot answer a holy life. Holiness remains the first work of the Holy Spirit. *The power of the Holy Spirit is the power of Holy Character.*

The power of the Holy Spirit is also the power of love. "The love of God is shed abroad in our hearts by the Holy Spirit which is given to us" (Rom. 5:5). Commissioner Brengle of the Salvation Army tells how he received the mighty baptism of the Spirit on January 9, 1885, at about nine o'clock in the morning. He states: "It was a Heaven of love that came into my heart. I walked out over the Boston Common before breakfast, weeping for joy and praising God. Oh, how I loved! In that hour I knew Jesus, and I loved Him till it seemed my heart would break in love. I loved the sparrows, I loved the dogs, I loved the horses, I loved the little urchins on the streets, I loved the strangers who hurried past me, I loved the Heathen—I loved the whole world."

Such ecstasy of course soon subsides into a calm and peaceful love, but the heart of the holiness imparted by the Spirit is holy love. Such love is irresistible and irrepressible—it is the motive power back of all the effective work for Christ. Without this love all our gifts are but as "sounding brass, or a tinkling cymbal." But clothed in that love the man with but little talent often becomes a wonder of power.

Most important of all, however, is the fact that the power we seek is the power of a Person: Often we are urged to ask God for more power to accomplish such and such a task. Actually what we need to do is to fall humbly on our knees before God and plead thus: "O Lord, take all sin from me. Teach me what it is that hinders Your coming. I will give up everything. Come, O Holy Spirit, come and take possession of me, and help me to win souls for Thee!" It is a mistake to seek power as such. *Power is the by-product of purity and of the Spirit's indwelling.* He has the power, and you have Him. Or better *He has you.* When we know that we have within us the indwelling presence of God, we become at once partakers of His omnipotence.

The inrushing of the Holy Spirit lifts life out of the shallows into the mighty oceanic fullness of God. "You will receive power when the Holy Spirit comes down on you." When He has come to dwell within, we are enabled to work and to witness, to live and to serve—*"not somehow, but triumphantly!"*

Paul speaks of "the supply of the Spirit of Jesus Christ" (Phil. 1:19). It is as though we were connected with the dynamo of the universe. The power of the Holy Spirit is not stored up in our little batteries; it flows in and through us as we maintain constant contact with God. In order to retain the dynamic of the Spirit we must continue to meet the conditions of *obedience and trust*. We can have His power only in line of His will. The electric train can draw the power from the wire only insofar as it follows the track. It can have the power to run along the rails, but it cannot have it to run into the neighboring farms and follow the capricious will of the engineer.

The Holy Spirit is given to them that obey Him (Acts 5:32). The obedience is a much larger thing than we sometimes imagine. It is not merely to keep us from doing wrong in some little contracted sphere; it is to understand and follow the whole will and purpose of God in the use of this divine endowment.

We cannot have it to please ourselves. We cannot have it to please ourselves even in the mode of Christian work. We can enjoy the fullness of the Spirit only insofar as we use this fullness for the work to which He has called us.

And to what work has God commissioned the Church? "Then you are to be my witnesses in Jerusalem throughout Judea and Samaria. Yes, even to the ends of the earth" (Acts 1:8). We can know the fullness of the Spirit's power only as we use it to give the gospel to the whole world. Only in the line of the world's evangelism and the fulfillment of our great trust can the Church of God ever realize the utmost meaning of the promise of Pentecost.

The last recorded words of Jesus Christ before His ascension were directed to His Church. They are in the form of a two-pronged promise: "You will receive power when the Holy Spirit comes down on you. Then you are to be my witnesses."

These two promises stand in relationship to one another as cause and effect. The power of the Holy Spirit coming upon them would produce effective witnesses. This is the very essence of Pentecost.

A witness is a giver of testimony, and a sanctified testimony was and is Christ's chosen instrument for evangelizing the world. Thus we see how vitally important a consistent testimony is to the building of the kingdom of God in every generation.

Trustworthy testimony is important in every area of human relationships. In a current newspaper a great bank asks this question in its advertisement, "Who keeps your safe-deposit keys? You do, and there are no duplicates." It is easy to see that a safe-deposit box in that bank is only as safe as the reliability of the testimony of the bank that "there are no duplicate keys" for unauthorized persons to use.

The Holy Spirit came at Pentecost with supernatural power; and He still operates through the faith of His people in His healing and wonderworking might, as a testimony to His word and a witness to an unbelieving world that He is still the living and present God.

These wonders also include the manifestations of His providence in answering prayer, removing difficulties, in breaking down barriers, in providing means for the carrying on of His cause, and in all those wonders of providence and grace of which so many examples have been given in recent years.

The Holy Spirit, who dwells in the Church, is the omnipotent executive of the Godhead, and is able to control the hearts of men, the elements of nature, and the events of providence, and to work together with His people, not only in the ordinary operations of His grace, but in the extraordinary manifestations of divine power that may best bear witness to His word and work.

We must trust Him for all the power we need for the carrying on of His work, and for the accomplishments of His will. If He dwells within us, He will work from without us. If He is pregnant in our hearts, He will show His dominion in the whole empire of His divine Power, both in the things that are in heaven, and the things that are on earth, and the things that are under the earth.

And thus it is in all of life's relationships. A home is founded on the marriage vow that husband and wife will be faithful to one another until death do them part. This testimony of faithfulness is the very cornerstone of the home when it is a reliable testimony. In the heart of the Christian who has not been baptized with the Spirit the testimony is often weakened by fear, cowardice, inconsistent living, and an "up and down" Christian experience. This is not only a very unsatisfactory life but it does great damage to the kingdom of God.

Thus we see the importance of the Pentecostal experience in its effect upon the testimony of the individual, and that in turn upon the task of the Church in winning men to Christ. A strong, positive, personal testimony is the basic instrument God is seeking for the successful evangelism in the home, the church, and the world. Pentecost is designed to produce this testimony in the life of the Spirit-filled Christian.

The power that was promised is, therefore, both the power to be and to do. We cannot live the Holy Servant's life consistently unless we have experienced Christ's fullness as well as His forgiveness. He must live freely within us so that He may work through us in conformity to His word. Such an experience of perfect love is nothing more or less than permitting the Holy Spirit to possess us entirely. *The experience of the Spirit's baptism, both initial crisis and continuing journey, is not so much a seeking for anything as it is a yielding to Someone.* We cannot live a holy life, but he will live that life in and through us if we will make ourselves entirely available to Him.

What a contrast in the effectiveness of the apostles' witness "before" and "after" Pentecost! For they accomplished more for God in one day after being filled with the Spirit than they had accomplished in three years of previous service.

Oh, how we need a spiritual breakthrough like that today! A modern Pentecost, a present-day infusion of a power greater than the human can generate, a power that will unify and cleanse and energize and embolden and make possible a new spiritual thrust into the enveloping, encroaching, and smothering secularism of our day!

We have placed our faith for spiritual and ecclesiastical success in bigger buildings and changed ritual, pastoral educational programs, and better public relations long enough. It is time we knelt in some "Upper Room" to tarry there in prayer until our hearts are melted in love and filled with the power of the Holy Spirit, which alone will vitalize our lives and energize our services and enable us to go out into a broken and corrupt world with the glad news of the gospel.

Oh, that God's people everywhere would experience a new unction, a new anointing, a new outpouring of the Holy Spirit!

8

Filled with the Spirit— Led by the Spirit

We have learned that the Holy Spirit is a Person, even God himself. Although His coming in fullness is a climactic and transforming experience, it is far more. *It is the start of a new and living relationship, which is possible only when we have surrendered to His sovereignty.* This is why the New Testament so often speaks of our relationship with the Spirit in very personal terms. Nowhere is this clearer than in the context of Paul's panorama of the works of the flesh (to be avoided) and the fruits of the Spirit (to be coveted). Here is performance at its peak! (Cf. Gal. 5:19-23.)

The wise apostle exhorted his Galatian converts to "live in accord with the Spirit and you will not yield to the cravings of the flesh" (verse 16). The metaphor of being "guided" and "led" by the Spirit is beautiful! It speaks of two persons, friends or lovers, out for a walk. Arm in arm, heart to heart, they journey together. So we will discover the power of the Spirit as we learn to be led by the Spirit. Only as we cultivate this *relationship* can we enjoy its fruits.

A few verses later Paul uses another concept, the meaning of which is unfortunately missed in some translations. *The Amplified New Testament* has captured the searching challenge: "If we live by the (Holy) Spirit, let us also walk by the Spirit—if by the (Holy) Spirit we have our life (in God), let us go forward walking the line, our conduct controlled by the Spirit" (Gal. 5:25).

Life by the Spirit is not simply aimless wandering hither and yon. Instead, it is a well-laid-out path toward the definite goal of Christlikeness. Here is disciplined living at its highest, not under the lash of law, but by the link of love.

We must always be open to the Spirit's guidance. It is those who are "led by the Spirit of God" who "are the sons of God" (Rom. 8:14). The guidance of the Spirit is of particular importance in confused and confusing times. When old certainties are being challenged, and stable ways of life are being blown away in a whirlwind of change, we must lean heavily on the promise of Jesus. "He shall guide you into all truths"—not mental furniture but reality in living.

If some of us in our zeal tend to get ahead of the Holy Spirit, others of us are in danger of lagging behind. We should endeavor to live where we can hear the smallest whisper of His voice. Sometimes it is not so easy to get His signals—then we must pray until the clamor of human desire subsides. But how sweet to know—and obey! At times, however, we may fail completely to discover that inner direction. What then? We may then safely seek the counsel of spiritually minded friends who can survey our situation objectively. The Spirit often guided the apostles through others who were acquainted with His way (Acts 11:28-30; 21:10-11, et al.).

There are occasions even when it would appear God leaves us to make our own decisions. As a wise parent delights in the maturing judgment of his son, so our Heavenly Father rejoices in our sanctified choices. But even in these choices we are being *indirectly* guided by the Spirit as we seek to make only those choices that would glorify God.

We need not doubt the faithfulness of the Spirit to help us at this point. Jesus assures us that "when he, the Spirit of truth, is come, he will guide you into all truths." The Book of Acts is the breathtaking account of the way in which the Holy Spirit guided the infant Church collectively and its members individually.

Being led by the Spirit is one of the hallmarks of personal relationship with God. But true guidance is never erratic. The urge to act hurriedly, without prayer and consideration, is never of God. We may truly be guided to act promptly, but never

Filled with the Spirit—Led by the Spirit

hastily, much less rashly. Moreover, we may be guided to act firmly, but never harshly. The freedom given in the Spirit never creates chaos. Quietness, calmness, a deep, unhurried assurance; these are the hallmarks of genuine guidance. Thus a Spirit-controlled, holy life is a well-balanced and divinely ordered life.

Holiness is wholeness, and a life lived in the fullness of the Spirit will be an intergrated whole. The Spirit teaches how to put things in the right order of priority. Unfortunately, some who claim to be led by the Spirit of God also claim that they can serve God in their own way. "Doing one's own thing" has become a modern fetish and multitudes are worshipping at its shrine. This has always been an inherent danger to pervert true "freedom in the Spirit."

In order to perceive what may have been received from the Holy Spirit, it must first be filtered through the human psyche. Therefore, it is subject to human error and misinterpretation. Only obedience to the teaching of the Holy Church, which guarantees our true discernment of the Spirit's will is one hundred percent infallible.

Freedom is always a temptation to declare one's independence, even of God, yet this is the very means by which the basis of freedom is destroyed. Only as men accept a responsible freedom, and relate themselves to God and His lawful representatives in obedience, is freedom in the Spirit guaranteed.

The implications of freedom are both challenging and frightening. Freedom implies power to destroy freedom. Every wrong choice closes doors along the way that God Himself will not batter down and that man cannot pry open.

In this light we can understand the familiar words of Scripture: "You shall know the truth, and the truth shall make you free"; "If the Son therefore shall make you free, you shall be free indeed"; "Where the Spirit of the Lord is, there is liberty."

The more we are responsive to the Spirit's guidance, the more will our personalities be delivered from the influences that enslave us; the more, also, will we discover we are able to establish bases for clear thinking, honest judgment, and willing love of God and neighbor according to the proper law. *Thus the Spirit-*

filled life is a life lived under bondage to Christ for the purpose of making man truly free. In this bondage, man strives for self-discipline, seeks instructions, heeds correction, and finally attains perfection.

This continuous cleansing of the inner disposition from sin by the purifying of the Holy Spirit is a recognizable and deeply personal experience that produces a consciousness of profound peace, and a sense of a closer fellowship in a divine partnership, and a great desire to be useful for Christ, and a cognizance of the unity of motivated love. This action of the Holy Spirit does not aim at suppressing man's efforts, but aims at sustaining him, and freeing him by enabling him to acquire effective control of his own interior liberty.

The great winsomeness of the Spirit-filled life lies in the uniqueness of a personality developing its full potential under the Spirit's guidance. "Where the Spirit of the Lord is, there is freedom" (2 Cor. 3:17), and there alone!

One of the main avenues by which our lives are guided by the Spirit is through prayer. He is "the Spirit of—supplications." "The Spirit too helps us in our weakness. For we do not know how to pray as we ought, but the Spirit himself makes intercession for us with groanings that cannot be expressed in speech. He who searches the hearts knows what the Spirit means, for the Spirit intercedes for the saints as God himself wills" (Rom. 8:26-27).

To be sure, none of us completely understands the working of intercession. But it is more important that we undertake it than that we understand it. It is particularly important that we be open to the Spirit in this vital area of the Christian life. One must avoid such tension as would block receptivity. We may be so intent on making our point with the Lord that we fail to listen to Him.

One of the most difficult areas of life for the conscientious, Spirit-filled Christian is that of guidance. Time after time people ask, "But how can I know what God's will is?" How eager we are to live wisely and well! Yet how difficult it can be to make right decisions. Not knowing beforehand what any day will bring

Filled with the Spirit—Led by the Spirit

to us, we wonder what will be best for us. What seems good now may not be so ten years hence.

God is the only One who knows the whole journey, so He is the One who can guide us successfully. Is His guidance available to us today? How do we recognize it? What are the conditions for receiving it?

God's willingness to guide us is assured and attested throughout the Bible. The Psalmist gives us God's promise in these words:

> I will instruct you and show you the
> way you should walk;
> I will counsel you, keeping my eyes
> on you.
> *(Ps. 32:8)*

The wisest of men, Solomon, has this to say:

> In all your ways be mindful of him,
> and he will make straight your paths.
> *(Prov. 3:6)*

Isaiah gives us this assurance:

> The Lord will guide you always
> and give you plenty even on the parched land.
> *(Isa. 58:11)*

God is ever seeking to guide us.. His infinite wisdom and knowledge are available to help us to live rightly today.

When our Lord was on earth, He made a promise that assures us that we can enjoy God's guidance today:

> I am the light of the world.
> No follower of mine shall ever walk in darkness,
> no, he shall possess the light of life.
> *(John 8:12)*

Jesus is with us wherever we go; therefore, we have not only guidance, but an infallible Guide.

How does God guide us? Principally through the Bible. A Psalmist points out:

> A lamp to my feet is your word,
> a light to my path.
> (Ps. 119:105)

God will never give guidance that contradicts His written Word. This guidance does not come from opening our Bible haphazardly and then accepting the first words we read as God's guidance for us. God will speak to us when we read it prayerfully and carefully each day, meditating upon what we read.

God has given us minds and expects us to use them. The Holy Spirit can direct us while we put our powers of thought, judgment, and common sense to the fullest use. He can flash in our minds what we need to know. He can work in our minds, guiding us to a right decision. As we consider the advantages of a course of action, looking at all the facts as impartially as we can, He can show us what will be best.

God can also guide us through our present circumstancess. Once we are sure that the Bible approves our course, and we have the inner assurance of the leading of the Holy Spirit, circumstances that all point the same way form a further indication of God's purpose for us.

Opportunity enters into God's guidance. As we go along the path of duty and come to a brick wall, we walk up to it. God will then either remove the wall that hinders our going ahead or tell us to go to the right or left. As Leonard Griffiths has put it: "Not for a moment would Paul explain the closing and openings of doors as mere human frustrations and opportunities; he would simply assume that the Spirit of God was guiding him in those directions and to those areas where his work would have the most enduring results."

Although God may give His guidance while we are on our

knees, He may give it through our friends. God has given wisdom and guidance to godly men and women. Their experience is invaluable. God can use that wisdom and experience to help us. Though we are always careful to check such guidance with plain instruction of Scripture, their advice may be the voice of God speaking to us.

We receive this guidance by asking God for it. This does not mean that crucial decisions are the only occasions for relying on God alone. Rather, seeking God's guidance is an attitude of life. We should seek it all the time. We may think we can distinguish between the great and small decisions, but we may err in our evaluation. Large doors turn on small hinges. We shall be habitually guided if we habitually seek God's guidance. Humbly and consistently seeking God's guidance will make us sensitive to God's activity in every aspect of life, not merely in its critical events.

Having sought it, we must expect it and look for it. Only when we expect it are we sensitive to the Holy Spirit's leading. Not only is this an evidence of our sincerity, but also it is the prayer of faith that God promises to answer. We are to seek it with sincerity, openness of mind, receptiveness of heart, and a will to follow it. God expects us to follow His guidance whether or not that guidance is what we would have chosen or is pleasing to us. God alone knows whether we shall follow His guidance.

It would be pointless for God to grant guidance unless we are prepared to obey it at all cost. Disobedience to clear direction will dull our perception of God's voice; continuous obedience will heighten and intensify that perception. When Scripture, inner conviction, and circumstances all agree, we need have no doubt about what we ought to do. We must obey.

God will guide us a day at a time. Often we should like to see the ultimate outcome of our decisions; we seldom do. God reveals one step; we take it. He then reveals the next; we take that. The longest journey is but a succession of steps.

Yes, we can make the right decisions today. Three attitudes destroy the "money-back guarantee" on God's gracious guidance:

Impatience wants God's way or my way, but whichever it is to be, it must be right now;

Ambivalence wants God's way and my way;

Selfishness wants my own way, with God's blessing and approval.

The presence of any one of these destroys the dynamic of the "willing, active, obedient will," to which God reveals His own desires!

Without this kind of walk our testimony becomes stagnant and meaningless, and we will soon discover we have the doctrine of the experience but not the vitality.

It is this being filled with the Spirit with all its wonderful effects that Paul commands the Ephesians to pursue from day to day, and from moment to moment. For the present continuous passive imperative of the Greek verb suggests a paraphrase like this: "Have yourselves continuously filled with the Spirit."

This Pauline exhortation shows very clearly that the baptism with the Spirit does not imply that one who receives this blessing automatically remains Spirit-filled. He must keep the doors of his heart and life wide open for the Holy Spirit. There must be unceasing prayer, a continuous, serious endeavor to bear the fruits of the Spirit in faithful obedience to the word. And anything that may grieve the Spirit must be denied.

If a Spirit-baptized believer becomes neglectful in any of these things, then the Holy Spirit begins to withdraw, slowly but surely. And He takes with Him the exuberant joy, the power to witness effectively, and the comfort of God's blessed nearness.

The command is still, "Be filled with the Spirit," but the word also comes to us clearly: "Since we live by the Spirit, let us follow the Spirit's lead." Dare we shake off the shackles of sameness, be done with the dullness of the daily drag, get out of the rut of routine, and begin the Spirit-filled, Spirit-led life? What a high adventure in God awaits us if we do!

9

The Laws of Fruit Bearing

This call to the Spirit-filled life is intended only for those who sincerely desire the best that God has. They have cut the shorelines that would hold them to the shore of sin and the shallows of worldliness. They have purposed to "launch out into the deep." Not only have they come to God with repentance and saving faith; they have died out to sin and self and have opened their hearts and lives to the sanctifying fullness of the Holy Spirit.

Having sold out to go with God, they consistently strive to cultivate a deep spirituality—or to grow deep in the Spirit. They recognize that even clean waters may be shallow, that the pure may be powerless. Their heart's desire is to be pleasing to Him who has called them "out of darkness into his marvellous light."

But deep spirituality is not cheaply won. Positively, there are disciplines of devotion to be cultivated. Negatively, there are dangers to be avoided. While problems arising directly from the carnal self are resolved by the abiding lordship of the Holy Spirit, the human self remains. St. Paul said, "What I do is discipline my own body and master it for fear that after having preached to others I myself should be rejected" (1 Cor. 9:27).

It is not easy to catalog all of the possible hindrances to growth in the Spirit; we may find a clue, however, in the New Testament description of the marks of a truly Spiritual, or Spirit-filled, Christian—known as "the fruits of the Spirit" (cf. Gal. 5:22-23).

Whatever in the way of attitude, tendencies, or dispositions would limit the manifestation of the Holy Spirit is certainly a hindrance to growth in the Spirit. The Lord has put us on notice as to points to guard. Let us now consider the laws of fruit bearing.

Of these numerous figures of speech used to portray life in the Spirit, one of the most expressive portrays the Christian as a fruit-bearing tree or plant or vine. St. Paul makes much of the fruit of the Spirit, and is very clear as to what the fruit is.

It is to Jesus, however, that we turn if we want to learn the laws of fruit bearing. These emerge with real clarity in the parable Jesus gives of the vine and the branches. This is recorded in John 15:1-8. Four laws of fruit bearing stand out.

The first law is that the *branches bear the fruit.* Fruit never appears on the vine, the stalk, or the tree. Fruit is always the product of the branch. This is the case whether it is a tall pear tree, a spreading grapevine, or a straight cornstalk. The limbs or branches produce the fruit.

Jesus portrays the Christian as a branch. The branches—you and I—bear the fruit.

We do the loving. We exude the joy. We demonstrate the peace. We are the ones who patiently endure. If the kindness, generosity, and faith appear, they appear in us. We will be the mild. We show what it means to be temperate, or disciplined. The branches bear the fruit.

Here a second law of fruit bearing appears. It is that *purging precedes productivity.* Jesus points out two things: fruitless branches are taken away; bearing branches are purged, that they may be still more fruitful.

There is a cleansing, a purging, a removing, an emptying out, as relates to Christians, before they can be maximum fruit bearers. It is "emptied of self" before "filled with Thee."

John the Baptist said of Jesus, "He it is who will baptize you in the Holy Spirit and fire. His winnowing-fan is in his hand, He will clear the threshing floor and gather his grain into the barn, but the Chaff he will burn in the unquenchable fire" (Matt. 3:11-12). There is first the purged floor, then the gathered wheat. The reason for the purging and pruning is greater productivity.

It is almost as if Jesus is saying that there is an alien strain in the vine. So we show bearing unkindness, joylessness, defeat, and such negations, to say nothing of the work of the flesh, which Paul contrasts with the Spirit's fruit. So purging is done.

The Laws of Fruit Bearing

Purging is done by the Father. This is not a spiritual do-it-yourself exercise. Purging precedes productivity.

The third law is staying constantly *refilled with the rivers of the Spirit*. We do not have to be an agriculturist to know that sufficient moisture is imperative to fruitfulness.

Jesus used the most familiar objects, the most ordinary events, the most customary practices, to illustrate and enforce spiritual truths. To set forth man's need of salvation, He spoke of thirst and of water. Jesus told the woman at the well He did not propose to give man simply a "drink of water" but to cause a spring, a fountain, to issue in his heart to quench the thirst of his spirit.

Many times the Old Testament refers to "living waters" in connection with the coming Christ (see Isa. 32:2;55:1; Zech. 12:10;23:1;14:4-8). The Book of Exodus speaks of the smitten rock from which came water to slake the people's thirst (17:6). The New Testament explicitly states that this "rock was Christ" (1 Cor. 10:4).

This Rock, Christ Jesus, had been smitten on Calvary and the precious Blood that flowed from His wounded side was the waters of salvation we would drink. The water was Christ's gift of the Holy Spirit.

Man is to experience personally this divine gift, for Jesus said to the woman of Samaria:

> But whoever drinks the water I give him
> will never be thirsty;
> No, the water I give
> shall become a fountain within him,
> leaping up to provide eternal life.
> *(John 4:14)*

The John 7 passage goes on to say, "Here he was referring to the Spirit, whom those that came to believe in him were to receive." It is through Christ that the Holy Spirit is conferred.

While Christ is the medium of the gift of the Spirit who satisfies man's spiritual thirst, it can be said in a secondary sense that believers are to share these "rivers of living water" with others.

In regeneration, the experience is a "spring of water welling up. . . ." This is for personal use. This "spring" is for our own practical benefit, to slake our own thirst, so that we shall never thirst again. Outward form is replaced by a new and inner source. Stagnant pools in the soul are transformed into a gushing well.

In the Spirit baptism it becomes "streams of living water," or "rivers," as some translations have it. The Spirit-filled life is characterized by abundance. What before was external and limited now becomes "internal, dynamic, out-flowing, and abundant." "The life that is open to God's fullness, reserved from ebb and fluctuation, and is independent of passing showers, with their pattering raindrops," writes F. B. Meyer.

"Streams of living water" sets forth the abundance of life that should flow from each Spirit-baptized Christian, who, having received out of God's fullness, should pass it on to a drought-stricken world. Just as a man comes and drinks of the water of life, he becomes himself a perennial source of life to others.

There is a great difference in measure between a "well" or a "spring" and "rivers" or "streams." The former is practically for one's own benefit, but the latter—the overflow—is for the blessings of others. There isn't a drop for the thirsty world until we get an experience that will cause us to overflow. *We will never bless anyone until we get something in us that we can't contain!* This brings us into the inexhaustible life.

These "torrents of living water" (H. R. Reynolds) are the outflow of the spiritual life. A. B. Simpson comments, in his book *The Holy Spirit*, volume 2, "This is the evidence that we are filled, because we cannot hold it longer, and fulfill ourselves in imparting the blessing to others. Like Ezekiel's river, it is flowing not in, but out pouring streams of blessing through the dry and desert places of life." Simpson continues: "It makes us simple, sweet, exuberant full-hearts. And enthusiastic for God, and our work and our words are the overflow of a life so deep and full that it brings its own witness, and it makes others long for the blessing that shines in our faces and speaks in our voices and springs in our glad and buoyant steps." He concludes: "Let us come to him and drink and drink again, and yet again, until our hearts are so full that we shall go out to find the sad, the sinning, and the suffering and comfort them with the comfort wherewith we ourselves are comforted of God."

The greatest satisfaction that can be known in this life is the privilege of communicating to others what has been received from the Risen Lord. We must make that unreserved consecration. When the soul has been placed in an eager, believing attitude toward Jesus, He will flood it with all the fullness of the Holy Spirit, and "streams of living water" will flow within.

If no fresh, deep spiritual stream runs through one's being, it is because he refuses to drink from the fountain that Jesus has opened. As we came initially to the Saviour, cisterns of stagnant water became "a fountain within leaping up to provide everlasting life." As we come again in total commitment, this "fountain within" gives way to "streams of living water" which flow from within.

As soon as life becomes positive, unselfish, and outflowing, it becomes streams of blessing in the life devoted to God and expended in blessing the world! One should not overlook the present, continuous tense of the verbs "come" and "drink." We are to keep on coming, and keep on drinking. This life-giving stream cannot diminish.

We do not subsist on one great surge of divine infilling, imperative as that is. The results of purging and infilling are not enough, valuable though they be. It is the constant contact, the "always abiding," that makes for meaningful fruit bearing.

Peter, John, and a host of those who had already been filled with the Spirit (Acts 2;4) were all filled "a fresh" (Acts 4:31). Clearly the most devout people of the early Church needed and received a fresh filling of the Spirit.

It was those wonderful seasons of "refreshing from the presence of the Lord" that kept the spiritual machinery of the early Church running smoothly. It was the inner grace that made possible that outer, radiant glow that attracted multitudes to the Church.

Such refreshing encouraged the Christians, helping them to realize that God was with them even in persecution. It gave the disciples courage to speak "the word of God with boldness." It brought renewed spiritual vitality.

Nothing will compensate for this divine infilling. Preparation, special training, unusual gifts and talents are desirable, but, apart from the Holy Spirit, they are like machinery without power, or guns with no powder to fire them.

Every Spirit-filled Christian should experience frequent outpourings of the Spirit. While there is one baptism of the Spirit, there are many refreshings along the way. We must have these seasons of refreshing if we are to keep fresh in our experience, blessed in our souls, victorious in the warfare with sin and Satan, and fruitful for the Kingdom of God.

One rainstorm makes a pond, but repeated rains make rivers. God wants to make rivers of His blessed Spirit. Are we willing to be channels? Each day we can be filled afresh with the Holy Spirit. There is a new infilling available for each new challenge. The Word admonishes us, "Be filled with the Spirit" (Eph. 5:18), so that our lives may bring blessing to others and glory to God.

In our day we hear of periods of drought. The devastation it causes is appalling. Cattle die, crops are ruined, and the land is unproductive. The people are forced to move to places where they can exist. The countryside is dotted with abandoned homes. All this creates a picture of desolation.

As frightful as that period of time always is, there is another "drought" that is much worse. It has much more far-reaching consequences. It is the absence of the Holy Spirit in one's life: He who refreshes with His presence, who makes life worth living.

When He is not present in one's life, there is a bleak barrenness. Life has no real meaning. It is just an existence. Others are not blessed by it.

We honor those who have made worthwhile contributions to us in the past. This is especially true of those who, through cen-

The Laws of Fruit Bearing

turies, have preserved the rich spiritual heritage that is ours. Preserving that heritage cost some of them their lives. They held life not dear unto themselves, so we have inherited the fruits of their richly sacrificial lives.

A life devoid of the fullness of the Holy Spirit cannot, and does not, produce the fruit of the Spirit. It is only with His presence that these are manifest. And Paul, in Galatians 5:22-23, points out that they are "manifest." In other words they are seen in the individual's life. He also makes it clear that they are there solely when He is in the heart and life.

This lack is not only a loss to the individual involved, but others receive no blessing. The fruit that affects our relationship with those about us are not present—love, patient endurance, kindness, and generosity. Many times the opposite is very much in evidence.

Refilling of God's great grace, of spiritual strength of power, and, at times, of the soft, tender encouragement of the Comforter, will come only as we take time to present our battle-worn, heavy-laden hearts to the Holy Spirit.

In this rushing, throbbing, hurrying world we, individually, and the Church collectively, need those times of seeking and receiving more of God's Spirit. It is the constant renewed sense of His presence that opens the way for a victorious, fruitful living of the Spirit-filled life.

There is one other law of fruit bearing, and the one on which the others hinge: *It is that fruitfulness depends on abiding.* Jesus tells us that it is not possible to bear fruit without abiding in Him and He in us. We cannot bear fruit of ourselves, apart from Him.

> Live in me, as I do in you.
> No more than a branch can bear fruit of itself
> apart from the Vine,
> can you bear fruit
> apart from me.
>
> *(Verse 4)*

The branch bears the fruits; this is clear. For the greatest productivity a purging is required; this is evident. The life-giving substance that makes the fruit possible must always come from Christ, the Vine. Hence, our continued contact with Him is imperative. As Jesus stated it, we are to abide in Him.

So we are always to be attached to the Vine. We are to abide in the Vine. We are to draw water—and sap—from the Vine.

Knowing this, shouldn't we expect every Christian, to stay in Him—the Way, the Truth, the Life to which He has called us? Who wants to be a dried-up castaway branch? I suspect no one does.

It is equally true, however, that few Christians look forward initially to being "pruned," or, as the marginal notes of some translations indicate, "cleansed."

Do we really want to know the truth, especially about ourselves? Jesus told us that in knowing the truth we would be freed to respond to God and others in the way intended by Him. He might have added that most of us would initially be frightened by such a call to God's progressive revelations of personal truth for each of His children. Freedom takes away our excuses for not being His people in deed as well as word.

It is critical to abide in Him, that we may receive in perfect and personal sequence the next truth, to do which He has for us. It is beautiful the way the Holy Spirit leads us into new areas of life adventure when we surrender to His healing journey, especially planned for each believer. He knows when and how to bring the situations, people, and lessons from His Word to produce the love, joy, peace, patience, and other fruit Jesus promised would result from our abiding.

Unfortunately, however, there are many who try to find a way to fit God's Word to their lives. Jesus' followers are known by their commitment to fit their lives to His Word.

When the Apostle Paul wrote Galatian Christians concerning their fruit of the Spirit, his call was to cultivate it all—"love, joy, peace, patience, generosity, faithfulness, mildness, self-control" (Gal. 5:22-23). In fact, he wrote of fruit, implying a unity, rather than fruits, suggesting separate life qualities.

The Laws of Fruit Bearing

How much easier it would be if we could pick by preference or choose the characteristic we find easiest to express because of learned emotions, habits, and motives within our human personality.

As abiders in Jesus, the whole cluster of fruit forms the seed of His love, the beginning—and the end—of our *balanced production* of the Spirit's fruit.

It must all grow in us—not just the qualities easiest to master. For that would be too readily explained as human rather than divine farming. Certainly the work of His Spirit in fruit growing is more evident for those qualities we were never able to cultivate effectively by our own efforts.

One of the most beautiful experiences in life is to appreciate the balance in God's world from sun to sea—from heaven to herd—from Him to me.

What perfect proportion Paul finds in the fruit cluster. From the exuberance of joy to the solemnity of self-control, the fire of love to the coolness of patience. This is truly God's fruit for all to see—the Spirit's union with us to produce Christ's balanced life in us. True life in the Spirit is one of discerning growth and abundant fruit bearing!

The vital question is: Are we abiding in Him? Are we experiencing the fresh, perennial anointings of the Holy Spirit? Only a poured-out or used vessel can be filled again. As stated, cleansing in the present tense is so beautifully illustrated in the present-tense verbs of 1 John 1:7.

The continuing and progressive ministry of the Holy Spirit enables us to add to our faith the seven growth-graces Peter spoke about: discernment, virtue, self-control, perseverance, piety, care for your brother, love (cf. 2 Peter 1:6-7).

He who hungers after the fruit of the Spirit is opening his whole life to the Spirit of God. The tragedy is that too many Christians are living in spiritual babyhood.

The fruitless Christian has lost his hunger for more of God. He has built a little shrine to yesterday, a particular high point of spiritual feeling, and sees not, nor longs for, a present reality of God's unfolding highway of holiness.

Our hunger for more of the Spirit is in direct relation to our spiritual discipline. When we begin to blur our ethical convictions with the world, we begin to lose our spiritual vision. Lady Julian, a spiritual giant of fourteenth-century England, wrote a meaningful prayer that underscores this truth: "O God, please give me three wounds; the wound of contrition, and the wound of compassion, and the wound of longing after Thee. This I ask without condition."

Are we wounded by our sorrow for our failures, our failure to love the lost world without condition of statistical improvement, or our failure to long after God, with a spiritual lump in our throat, and ache for His continuing fullness?

The laws of fruit bearing remind me of a story once heard: A man stood in desperation at the edge of a mountain precipice and cried out to God, "More of You, more of You, more of You." And in the silence of the mountain passes he heard the echo coming back: "More of you, more of you, more of you."

This is what Christ means by abiding!

10

The Fruit of the Spirit: Love

All of us, after committing ourselves to Christ, continue to experience some degree of difficulty in believing the truth of our relation to Him.

Psychologists have observed a number of "defense mechanisms" designed to protect our self-image against contrary evidence and the anxiety that self-knowledge often produces. These include such strategies as attributing our feelings to others (projection) and giving less than honest reasons for our actions (rationalization).

It is also possible that we have not heard the truth about a particular area of life experience. Maybe we have heard but not received the new word in obedient faith. All our faulty ways of thinking about ourselves and relating to others obviously do not get lost or cleansed in our spiritual crisis experiences. We thank God that He brings new life and cleanses desires, giving Him control to *continually accomplish* His purpose and our best in us.

Step by step, just as Jesus promised,

The Paraclete, the Holy Spirit
whom the Father will send in My name,
will instruct you in everything,
and remind you of all that I have told you.
(John 14:26)

In St. Paul's call for complete surrender, given to Roman Christians, he also emphasized the transformation that is to take place by the renewing of our minds, ". . . so that you may judge what is God's will, what is good, pleasing and perfect" (Rom. 12:2).

Practically, our renewal works like this: Consider the human need, some say the most profound we have, to be unconditionally loved while perfectly known. If we are "loved" without self-disclosure, we can always say, "But if they only knew. . . ." Many Christians "believe" that God in Christ Jesus demonstrated this in dying to save us, yet continue to "believe" that they are inferior, worthless, and unlovable as seen by Him and others.

Logically, we can't faithfully obey John 3:16-17, Romans 8:38-39, and other such Biblical truths concerning God's perfect and constant love for us while continuing to "believe" the lie that we are losers with God and others.

But emotionally, we can and do hold on to such nonsense. We must have a convincing encounter with another believer living in Him who puts flesh and blood to this truth in our lives before we will give up such self-defeating lies.

It is probably right to say that most of us have heard all the right words of instruction about love among the brothers. We simply need to experience more of this fruit of the Spirit in our relationships. Jesus said this would glorify His Father and we would thus prove to be His disciples.

For, essentially, the central message of a Spirit-filled life is the message of love.

When we understand love as Paul describes it in 1 Corinthians 13, it comes close to being the very heart and soul of true Christianity, viewed from both God's side and ours.

Students of the New Testament have puzzled over the strange grammar in Galatians 5:22-23: "The fruit of the Spirit is love, joy, peace, patient endurance, kindness, generosity, faith, mildness, and chastity."

It would sound as if Paul should have written, "The fruit of the Spirit *are*," or "The *fruits* of the Spirit are."

There are two ideas about what lies behind this manner of speaking—and both of them may be right.

One is that the measure of the indwelling of the Holy Spirit is not a series of disconnected virtues, any one of which might exist in isolation from the others. To say, "The fruit of the

The Fruit of the Spirit: Love

Spirit *is*" shows that the fruit of the Spirit constitutes an indivisible whole, so interrelated as to be inseparable.

This is in complete contrast to the gifts of the Spirit.

Of the gifts, Paul writes, "To each person the manifestation of the Spirit is given for the common good" (1 Cor. 12:7). "To one is given by the Spirit the word of wisdom . . . to another the word of knowledge . . . to another faith . . . to another the gifts of healing," and so on through the list (verses 8-10). And "one and the same Spirit who produces all these gifts, distributing them to each as He wills" (verse 11).

But the graces listed in Galatians 5 are not divisible. It is not that one person is given love, another joy, another peace, another patience, another kindness. All belong together and all grow together.

Thus, the Holy Spirit is the Gift in Person: the Gift whom the Father and the Son give to each other, and also the Gift made to our souls by the Father and the Son. It is in giving us the Holy Spirit that the Father and the Son give themselves to us. We possess Him as their supreme Gift, the Gift who is the pledge and guarantee of all the other gifts of their love—the gift of charity. The invisible mission of the Divine Persons evokes, at once, the idea of a resemblance to the Person sent—a resemblance to the personal qualities that the Person possesses as of Himself. This resemblance is effected in our souls by a gift that is, as it were, the imprint of this Divine Person.

This should make us realize, with a rush of joy and gratitude, what the nature of this life of love is and must be, to which we are called. For it is this realization—and this response—within us that causes the growth of charity and increase of love, marking us with the same mission as the Holy Spirit. It is a *state of oblation* that the Holy Spirit comes to impress on us. He comes to awaken our souls, in order to purify them from all selfishness, and to fix them with a *permanent tendency to give.*

God's kind of love in us is more than a romantic feeling. It is a commitment, an undeviating purpose that strives always for the good of the beloved.

Human love is liking; God's kind of love is caring—and there is a world of difference between the two! God's kind of love can care tremendously about people even while it doesn't like what they do. Our problem is that we so often fail in caring about those we don't like.

God's kind of love in us may be pure and even "perfect" in that it excludes all rivals, and still be growing and deepening day by day.

The other understanding of Galatians 5:22 has equal merit. It hears Paul as saying, "The fruit of the Spirit is love" (period). That love is joyful, serene, patient, kind, good, faithful, gentle, and temperate.

Here we have a striking parallel with 1 Corinthians 13:4-7: "Love is patient; love is kind. Love is not jealous, it does not put on airs, it is not snobbish. Love is never rude, it is not self-seeking, it is not prone to anger; neither does it brood over injuries. Love does not rejoice in what is wrong but rejoices with the truth. There is no limit to love's forbearance, to its trust, its hope, its power to endure."

How better could one describe the Christlikeness that is the essence of the Spirit-filled life? By the same token, "Who is sufficient for these things?"

Certainly no one in himself could rightly claim to have fathomed "the breadth, and length, and depth" of "the love of Christ which surpasses all knowledge" (Eph. 3:19-19). It is only as "the love of God has been poured out within our hearts through the Holy Spirit who was given to us" (Rom. 5:5) that sentences like these become more than just words.

Theologians tell us that the Holy Spirit is the mutual love of the Father and of the Son, in the bosom of the Holy Trinity. He is the fruit of their love, but, for us, He is also the pledge of their love. It is He who keeps us united to the Father, and to the Son, in love. It is through Him that the Father and the Son are united with us, in order to make us communicate, through Him, in their life of love. This is the paradox of an imperfect perfection that is the basis of a Spirit-filled life.

For the logic of love is the fact that love is capable of being

The Fruit of the Spirit: Love

at the same time perfect and yet growing. Indeed, if it does not grow, it is not perfect—for love that does not deepen in devotion and increase in range is fast on the way to becoming indifference or downright aversion.

To be more spiritual, in the final word, is to manifest more of the nature of God, and "God is love." The motive and accent of Christ's words were always love. Even when He was severely strict in condemning sin and hypocrisy among the scribes and Pharisees, His words were couched in love.

We all know by experience that this kind of love that loves the sinner in spite of his sin is made possible only through love of God in the human heart. No person can put on this love at his own choosing. It is only when the Lord comes to live and rule in our hearts that the love of God is shed abroad in our hearts by the Holy Spirit. Christian love springs to life when Christ fully indwells the heart of one who has given himself absolutely to Him. *To lose love is to lose God!*

Love does not come by will power. Love comes by a Presence. That Presence cannot be legislated or legalized. It is the very spirit of Jesus Christ, whose purpose is to fill man's minds and hearts with His love.

Natural or human love can never be developed into divine love. For our natural love, regardless of culture and refinement, is self-centered. This disposition is the tragic result of Adam's sin. Divine love becomes ours only in the work of redemption. As Christ came into the world from the outside, so He with His love must come into our lives from outside our natural capacities. And when He comes, our loves are different.

God's word speaks of his love as a gift of grace. How beautifully true are the words of John:

> See what love the Father has bestowed on us
> in letting us be called the Children of God!
> *(1 John 3:1)*

It is not given to the mystic elite. Rather it is for all who by faith know the Saviour's forgiveness. Love is never produced by struggling. Love is an effect. We receive love when we receive God. Perfect love means that we have opened all avenues of our being, and that He has come and taken possession of every chamber of our hearts.

To love God with all the heart, with all the soul, and with all the mind, and with all the strength, and to love "one's neighbor as himself" is to fulfill the greatest of all commandments and exceed mere pretense of hollow profession (cf. Mark 12:28).

It is through the divine gift of Charity that we possess the Holy Spirit whom we have in common with the other members of the Mystical Body of Christ. It is, indeed, the Holy Spirit that, rising superior to all divisions of races and of peoples and sweeping together all space and all time, forms the profound unity of the Mystical Body. Thus a genuine love for God is the bond of communion that we share with our families and our brothers and sisters in Christ. Finally, it is our love for God Himself that demands that we should taste the joy of sharing with all the other members the riches of Christ. *For joy is the fruit of love.*

Love impels, forces, spurs, binds, drives, and obliges the Christian in his walk with God. Only the presence of Christ is desired, only His will is sought, and only His works count.

Love knows no limit to its endurance, no end to its trust, no fading of its hope; it can outlast anything. It is the one thing that still stands when all else has fallen.

Love knows one obstacle: the overwhelming care of self. Egoism in all its forms is a strong screen interposing itself between the soul and God, the Christian and his brothers. This is why we find the Saviour the supreme example of love—which is the first fruit of the Spirit. His love was diffused without hindrance. His love was like a glowing furnace that sat everything aflame with its spreading sparks, for He is the Light of the world.

As He pours out His love into all hearts, and lets His glance fall as flames of fire, so He moves us in turn to the brotherly service of the world that enlightens and the love that shares. The richness of Christ's sharing includes all of us whom He has known and loved as He leans on the Heart of the Father. This is what

The Fruit of the Spirit: Love

our testimony means; this is the kind of love we share, or the love of Christ is not in us!

Christian love is therefore not primarily an emotion but a *principle of unselfish action*. It may or may not be accompanied by personal affection or admiration. Christians can give themselves in unselfish concern for the highest good of those whose lives are offensive to them, or whose attitudes repel them, or who are their declared enemies.

Holy love includes a worldwide compassion for all men. We are brothers—creatures of one God—and all purchased by the same sacrifice on Calvary. Charity does not stop at the end of one's lot, at the end of the block, at the end of the city limits of one's particular town, at the edge of one's own race, at the border of one's economic class, or even at the close of this generation. We cannot escape our involvement in the heartaches of the world if we would produce the fruit of the Spirit!

It can only be a giving and forgiving love, rendering service, not self-seeking and vainglorious. Such a love would seem to disperse the centering of the inward-turning witness. But the very opposite is true. The more deeply love expresses itself, and the more selflessly it espouses the cause of others, the more interior it becomes both to itself and to others. It is by giving that love is enriched. It is by serving that it is ennobled. Love's nature is to bestow itself. Love follows the lead of the Risen One!

The miracle of redemption is that God turns us, the loveless ones, into the standard of Himself, the loving One, by coming to abide in us and being in us what we cannot be ourselves.

This love of God burning in our hearts is very costly. It is the kind of love that brings soul burden and concern to the human heart. It is the kind of love that often produces periods of fasting when the desire for good is gone. It is the kind of love that drives one to his knees and eventuates in solitary and sometimes long prayer vigils. It is the kind of love that is not deterred by excess or alibis, and knows no barriers, and that will find a way to express and manifest itself in trying to win the lost to Jesus. It is the kind of love that St. Paul exhorts us to seek as "the way which surpasses all others."

This is love made perfect. But we must remember that perfect love does not ensure perfect practice. It would be a mistake for me to imply that it does. What may be ensured is a perfect purpose, and in the perfection of that holy purpose, *constantly renewed by the Holy Spirit, the practice will be constantly corrected upward.*

This love becomes the cause of our rejoicing. It rejoices in the redemptive possession that conquers all sin; it is His personal presence. Love alone makes our words significant. Love alone makes our works of the same quality as His work, and we have joy in tribulation. Men without Christ respond to this love when they cannot understand what we say. It demonstrates its own language of redemption.

Because the heart and soul of the Christian experience is the love of God shed abroad in our hearts by the Holy Spirit, a censorious and faultfinding spirit will sap the vitality and ultimately destroy the life within. Bitterness, resentment, or animosity of any kind is a prime peril to the Spirit-filled life. John says He is love. He is kind to the ungrateful and the selfish. He makes His sun rise on the evil and on the good, and sends rain on the just and on the unjust. He never changes His love for man, no matter what man's response is. As Jesus says, it's easy to love those who love you. But Jesus tells us to love even our enemies, to "be merciful, even as your Father is merciful."

When we repeat the Lord's prayer we are striving for this kind of attitude: that we will forgive others their feelings as the Father has forgiven us. As we are forgiven, so must we develop and maintain the power to forgive.

It is necessary that love of enemies must always be initiated by the person who has been wronged. Love of enemies does not mean ignoring what has been done or putting a false label on an evil act. It means, rather, that the evil act will no longer remain a barrier to the love relationship. Love of enemies means forgiveness, and forgiveness means a reconciliation—a coming together again, the seeking of peaceful means for the settling of differences.

Jesus suggests that the only viable response to wrong done to

The Fruit of the Spirit: Love

us is forgiveness. It relaxes tension and sets us free from bitter debilitataing thoughts. It opens the door for the renewal of broken human relationships and enables us to think with clarity and understanding.

Forgiveness is not a matter of saying lightly, "Don't mention it," and gracefully leading the conversation to another subject. It is costly and painful. Calvary is proof to us that to forgive offenses is a costly and painful thing even for God. Nothing else, however, can make wrong things right and let God's healing grace into the situation.

Animosity and bitterness in us keep God at arm's length. God cannot invade the mind of an angry man or woman to forgive the anger and relieve the tension. He cannot forgive our follies and our sins while we cling to resentment against others. But in the moment that we forgive, there is a gentle invasion of God's forgiveness that restores our own right-mindedness. Our hope for forgiveness hinges on our willingness to forgive.

Today we live in a world whose unhealed wounds are constantly being torn open afresh. We see the failures of humankind and the bankruptcy of statesmanship. We shrink at the cutting edge of sorrow, and sin seems so immense that no single mind can grasp its total bitterness and tragedy. Our duty as Spirit-filled Christians in an un-Christian world is to display the truth in word and deed that "the greatest of these is love." We must demonstrate perfect love in the face of abuse and oppression.

God has already given us a model of that kind of forgiving grace. Though because of our sin we deserved punishment, because of His grace, or undeserved favor, we receive forgiveness. Just as His forgiveness of our sins is an act of grace, so our forgiveness of others is an act of grace. It is the inward work of the Holy Spirit that makes the difference. He helps us grow in the spirit of forgiveness. He supplies within us grace sufficient to forgive any wrong by any person anytime. And the Holy Spirit, given the opportunity, will mature that spiritual grace within us.

Psychologically, when resentment alienates us from other persons, it becomes difficult to give or receive evidence of healthy, wholesome friendship. Healing begins with a healing personality.

Spiritually, it would be a moral monstrosity to receive God's forgiveness for all our sins and yet refuse to forgive the wrongs done against us. God is ready to forgive, but an unforgiving spirit is a barrier of our own making to His forgiveness.

So it is for such good reasons that Jesus taught unlimited forgiveness. Growing in the spirit of forgiveness makes one a healing personality who can lovingly restore broken relationships. Is there any sin that Christ will not forgive? No, there is not! Is there any wrong that the person in Christ will not forgive? No, there is not! As the Spirit lives within us, we can say, "By the grace of God I am forgiven—and by the grace of God I will forgive." As John Oxenham declared, "Love ever gives, forgives, outlives; and ever stands with open hands: and, while it lives, it gives—for this is love's prerogative: to give, and give, and give!" Who would not pray for more love such as this!

11

The Fruit of Joy and Peace

A truly Spirit-filled Christian has always been a joyful Christian. No one can read the Bible or the lives of the Saints without hearing the constant note of joy running all through the record. True, there were seasons of defeat and despair. But the joy of the Lord has always been one of the greatest sources of strength in the Christian life.

That joy is the natural accompaniment of salvation is the plain teaching of the Scriptures. In Psalm 50, David prayed, "Restore unto me the joy of salvation." When he sinned, David lost something he wished restored when his relationship to God was renewed. In Galatians 5:22, Paul teaches that joy is as much a fruit of the Spirit as is love. In Romans 14:17, we read that "the kingdom of God is . . . joy that is given by the Holy Spirit." Romans 15:13 constitutes a prayer: "So my God, the Source of hope, fill you with all joy and peace in believing." Thessalonians 1:6 indicates that the Thessalonians received the Word "in much affliction" but "with joy in the Holy Spirit."

Add to these Scriptures the words of Christ: "These things I have spoken to you, that my joy be in you, and your joy may be filled," and the conclusion is that joy is the natural accompaniment of one's relationship with God through Christ.

Whether or not a person is totally committed to God determines whether that person finds real joy and fulfillment in serving the Lord. Most miserable of people are those who are halfhearted in their devotion to God; they know neither the fleeting pleasures of sin nor the rewards of the approbation of the people of God. Total commitment becomes real only as we develop such a deep appreciation for Christ that we are eager to take the adventurous risk with Him.

This joy, however, is not to be confused with pleasure or with what the world calls "happiness." Pleasure is a thing of the senses. Joy is an attitude of the soul. Happiness is closely related to happenings, and depends to a large extent on time and chance. Joy can be gloriously independent of circumstances. Because it is an import from the world beyond and not native to earth, the supply of joy does not depend on what is happening in this world.

One of the wonders of spiritual joy is that it may be experienced in times of sorrow. How little true spiritual joy has in common with the natural high feelings that go by the same name is shown by what happened after the Ascension. In Luke 24:52 we read, "They fell down to do him reverence, then returned to Jerusalem filled with joy." In this report, cause and effect seem to have abandoned their natural usage. The Lord had withdrawn from the sight of His faithful followers, but left joy in their hearts. Thus, their very consolation was in the pain of their parting!

It is not that the joyful disciples descending from Mount Olivet did not feel the separation, just as we may feel the painful separation from a loved one. But their hearts, which were possessed and enlightened by Christ, were wiser than their senses. In the wisdom of their burning hearts they realized that the departure of the Lord, while it deprived them of His sensible company, bore with it the assurance of His return and abiding nearness: "I go and I come to you." This knowledge overtook the pain before it could overwhelm them and changed it to an enlightened joy.

Joy breaks through from dark backgrounds of sadness. It is a joy purified by tears, joy overcoming pain and able to ripen in purity and perfection.

Yes, God's people are able to rejoice in trouble. Even tests and spiritual pressure cannot destroy the joy of the Lord. We may rejoice with joy unspeakable and full of glory while in heaviness through manifold temptations (1 Peter 1:6-8), because faith sees the end of the testing to be glorious. It knows that the Christian would not be the disciple of His Master if he sought to stand aside from the sufferings of the world and avoid all its human dramas. On the contrary, he knows he must also take on himself the burden of the Cross, which His Master carried alone, two thousand years ago.

Thus, Christian joy reaches out even into sorrow, and has its role to play there; for joy and sorrow are perfectly compatible, though they appear to be contradictory one to the other. Indeed, opposition and persecutions and trials, when embraced for love of Christ, but fan the flame of joy, and cause it to burn brighter.

Surrender to depression and moodiness is a sure blockage to the flow of joy that should emit from the Spirit-filled Christian. That there will be seasons of heaviness through trial and temptation is an admitted fact. But no truly Spirit-filled Christian is helpless in the face of moods. To surrender to them is to give unnecessary opportunity to the devil to get in his work of destruction.

The Lord has given us joy to be our strength. As Karl Barth has said, "The glory of God is also his over-flowing, self-communicating joy." Without joy, there is no spirituality. Joy, in fact, is love's response in faith to the presence of God in Christ, made real to us by the Holy Spirit.

Our most difficult trials only serve to reveal to us the all-sufficiency of our wonderful Lord and Saviour.

Joy, the Saviour, and salvation from all sin, are inseparable to the child of God.

God indeed is my Savior,
I am confident and unafraid.
My strength and my courage is the Lord,
and he has been my saviour.

With joy you will draw water
at the fountain of salvation. . . .
(Isa. 12:2-3)

The joy of the Lord may be deep and abiding, quite as a placid lake. Or it may be as bubbling and effervescent as an artesian well. It is not dependent on physical well-being. It is constant, for it is the gift and the fruit of the Holy Spirit.

Since joy is the fruit of the Spirit, it is difficult if not impossible to be counting one's blessings, realizing the wonder and miracle of the love of God, and remain long in the fog of doubt and depression. When everything falls down around our heads and our finest dreams and aspirations burst like bubbles or crumble like ashes at our feet, the joy of the Lord is our strength, nourishment, and sustenance.

A joyless person is usually living in the past. Only the future holds out hope. Cluttering up today with yesterday's failures, disappointments, sorrows, and sins can only rob today of its radiance. St. Paul says, "Brothers, I do not think of myself as having reached the finish line. I give no thought to what lies behind but push on to what is ahead. My entire attention is on the finish line as I run toward the prize to which God calls me—life on high in Christ Jesus" (Phil. 3:13-14). Yesterday's clay has already hardened. Today's is still workable. Trying to relive, rethink, and resuffer our yesterdays only produces misery. Joy is found in doing God's will today and planning to do it tomorrow.

There are, however, prerequisites to possessing the joy of the Lord. Perfect joy means joy that *gives*. Because it stems from the gracious self-communication of Christ, a gift from His glory, Christian joy dwells in the will to communicate. The more we lift our eyes to Christ, the Father of the world to come, above the distorted shapes of passing time, the more keenly we are drawn to joy.

It is a joy that bears the stamp of giving, of spending the self. To enlighten others, it must of course first transform itself. This is right in the natural feeling of joy, all wrapped up in itself. Joy is repose in fulfilled and blessed inwardness, but to have promise for the future it must take on another form, one organically in touch with the world about it. *It must dis-close itself*. What joy knows and cherishes as its inner strength must be made clear to everyone.

This it does when it becomes kindness, for kindness is joy

The Fruit of Joy and Peace

that looks to fellow men and reaches out to them and is therefore the perfection of joy. It is not without significance that Apocalyptic images of happiness in the light of the Lamb are always images of community. The happy "I" is but the beginning of joy; its goal is the "We" showered with the same singular happiness.

This is the reason why self-forgetfulness is a necessity if we want to enjoy mental health and happiness. Happiness comes through sharing, and this the self-centered person cannot do. He is so involved with his own fatigue, aches and pains, he cannot listen to the concerns of others.

Nor can he see himself as others see him. He may wonder why people don't care to be around him, why he isn't as popular as he would like to be. He needs to realize that people want to be around those who are happy, those who make them feel better, those who have something to give and joy to share.

The way out of self-centeredness is not easy. Stopford A. Brooke said: "It is hard, when we are the victims of feelings which eat at our heart day and night, to force ourselves into the life of giving, of doing little things for others, or stepping out of our reserve, of conquering our wish for solitude, of going to cheer and comfort those who are dependent upon us, of surrendering our pride, of doing a little good here and there when we had rather do big things; but it is the true way to get rid of the enslaving dominion of the greater passions.

"It will bring joy and peace at last, for it is at the root of God's peace. It was the calm of Christ, and when He left us His last legacy of peace, He left the means of it in the New commandment: 'Love one another as I have loved you.'"

The joy of the Lord is also *plenteous*. "These things I have spoken to you, that your joy may be filled." The term means "complete," fully satisfying. Christian joy is indeed full-orbed and complete. It includes the joy of pardon, of sins forgiven. The heavy load of guilt and condemnation is lifted. Truly "blessed is he whose transgression is forgiven, whose sin is covered" (Ps. 32:1). Christian joy is the joy of purity, of a heart washed and made white in the "fountain opeend for sin and uncleanness"

(Zech. 13:1). When Jesus prayed for the sanctification of His disciples, one of the reasons He gave was "that they may share my joy completely."

Such joy is naturally winsome and attractive. A joyful person is radiant and magnetic. In a world full of sorrow and disappointment, gladness and glow have a wonderful drawing power. Is it any wonder that the early Christians, "filled with joy, and with the Holy Spirit" (Acts 13:52), were all but irresistible to the people of their day?

Such joy as this is the joy of a wonderful prospect. But we are yet strangers and pilgrims on earth, and our joy is not comparable in intensity with the joy of Heaven. Here we must savor joy, not in the direct and immediate Vision of Glory, but in the light that is also the twilight of faith. The final joy comes to those who faithfully endure the sufferings of Christ, so that, as Peter says, "When his glory shall be revealed, you may be glad as with exceeding joy." His invitation to glory is an invitation to "enter thou into the joy of the Lord."

With all of this, there seems to be dearth of joy among Christians. For all that God has done for us, there is still little rejoicing. Nor should any of us point the finger at any other. For joy is contagious and each and any one of us can add to the radiance by the divine glow in his own heart.

But joy does not come by simply wishing for it. If Christian joy has permanence, it is because its Author is always near; under the garment of the gift, the presence of the Giver is tangible. Thus joy, like all else in the spiritual life, is subject to divine principle and laws. In order that our lives may be illuminated with light and filled with joy, the glance of the Glorified Christ must rest upon us. The gladness God puts in our hearts as His people increases as we give expression in praise.

Students of human nature have long known that any emotion is increased as it is expressed. The surest way to kill joy is to smother it. The best way to increase it is to express it.

Finally, perfect joy means enthusiastic joy. It is significant that joy is counted among the fruits ripened by the breath of the Holy Spirit. It must be a spiritual joy, in harmony with its origin. Then it is itself and bursts with the power that slumbered before. It is only when we are deeply stirred that we know how to give place to the Christ within us.

When we are trembling with rapture we overcome ourselves to re-express in Christ our separate identities and to subject to His yoke our urge to be self-made. In that instant, the very stream of our life is reversed; a feeling for the eternal divinely shaped life takes hold on us. Our beggar's rags, the garb as exiles from the Lord (cf. 2 Cor. 5:6), fall from us and we realize that we are guests. Every question, every wish is mute. For the Holy Spirit who has come over us, chooses us, and runs through our soul, is greater than anything we were going to ask or could have wished.

Joy is the infallible truth of God's presence, and a deep and abiding joy is one of the distinguishing hallmarks of Pentecostal spirituality. Let us therefore enter into joy by saying in truth, "Thank You, Father."

THE GIFT OF PEACE

The peace of God is the poise and serenity of trust. In a jittery, jumpy age, a person at peace with God, with himself, and with his circumstances is rare enough to stand out like a beacon. And this is just what the Spirit-filled Christian is called to be—a beacon of light in a sin-darkened world! The only permanent cure for a disturbed and turbulent spirit is the peace of God that passeth all understanding.

But the peace for which men presently strive remains elusive because they seek it apart from God. We must first seek His holy will; then peace subdues every disturbing circumstance.

The Spirit speaks peace to the surprising present—to the trials, sufferings, the temptations, the threats of living in an unfriendly world. Come what may, "We know that God makes all things work together for the good of those who have been called according to his decree."

When Christ was about to ascend to the Father, He assured

His disciples, "Peace I leave with you, my peace I give unto you." St. Paul tells us that it is the fruit of the Holy Spirit.

Among the fruits of the Spirit enumerated in the letter to the Galatians, peace follows joy and both are promised as the legacy of the departing Lord. Together with joy, peace is the shared glory of the Glorified Christ. Peace, however, is distinguished from joy in its relationship to the content of the gifts and to their Giver. If joy is the inward reflection of His glory, peace is His precious presence among all whom His joy animates. So peace completes the work of joy.

Peace is the seal of the sanctifying Spirit bearing witness with man's spirit that rebellion has ceased and resignation has come.

> A Nation of firm purpose you keep in peace,
> in peace, for its trust in you.
> (Isa. 26:3)

Thus peace is paramount where mental contentment, emotional confidence, and spiritual confirmation exist unwavering within one of God's children. Here is the curse: "A double-minded man is unstable in all his ways." But here is the cure: "Draw close to God, and he will draw close to you. Cleanse your hands, you sinners; purify your hearts, you back sliders" (James 4:8).

It is interesting to note the frequency of Biblical statements directly connecting holiness and peace, such as "The Kingdom of God is not a matter of eating or drinking, but of justice, peace, and the joy that is given by the Holy Spirit" (Rom. 14:17). "The fruit of the Spirit is . . . peace" (Gal. 5:22). "May the God of peace make you perfect in holiness" (Thess. 5:23).

It is not surprising then that the Psalmist cried out of a full heart,

> Those who love your law have
> great peace,
> and for them there is no
> stumbling block.
> (Ps. 119:165)

The Fruit of Joy and Peace

Peace for today comes from the purity of a clear conscience, a sanctified life of faithful obedience to God's will.

"May the God of peace make you perfect in holiness. May he preserve you whole and entire, spirit, soul, and body, irreproachable at the coming of our Lord Jesus Christ. He who calls us is trustworthy, therefore he will do it" (Thess. 5:23). Thus did Paul see the intimate relationship between God's peace for us and the purity of our living for Him.

In the new covenant, the first time we see this relationship is in Jesus' teaching about progression in the disciple's spiritual life. In the Beatitudes (cf. Matt. 5:3-12), He sequentially coupled the pure in heart with the happy state of being peacemakers, a consequence of purity in our life purpose.

The issue is simple. How can we speak peace to another until we know the motivation of our own life?

The purity of a clear conscience is the prescription for personal peace. We can be made glad to expose our life to the light of the Son.

But if we walk in light,
as he is in the light,
we have fellowship with one another,
and the blood of his Son Jesus cleanses us
from all sin.
(1 John 1:7)

The promise is only to those who love God's law, not simply those who endure it, but to those who love. To love God's will for our lives until it becomes primary with us results in great peace—not just peace, but great peace. Nothing brings peace like surrender to God, abandonment to self, and the consecration of one's all to the Christian cause. No tranquility ever has been known to rise above such peace. No joy, happiness, or elation has ever brought to the heart of man the "peace of God, which passeth all understanding."

The test here is: Do we truly love God's law? Do we seek His testimonies? Do we follow His precepts? For there is real heart peace only through complete surrender to the Holy Spirit in sanctification of heart and life. If we reject its Author, peace is aborted. In God it has origin, through Jesus it has fruition, and by the Holy Spirit it has application. If we refuse its principles, peace is prohibitive. The readiness for peace, the longing for the peace, and the right dispositions will prepare the heart for peace; the gift of it must be bestowed by Christ.

It is also true that if we live in peace we shall no longer live for ourselves. Something truly great has come down to us and taken away all narrow self-seeking. At home now in Christ we are in harmony with all creation; nothing can trouble us. Our fellowmen, whom Christ has bought, we bear wrapped in our hearts; nothing they can do can embitter us. Possessed by Christ, we know that we are one with the image of Christ; nothing can separate us from His love.

Where peace reigns the human heart has passed from seeking to finding, from asking to knowledge, from desire to possession. There may never come relief from the staggering problems of life, respite from the titanic responsibilities, or redress from legitimate obligations incurred in previous days. Yet in holiness of heart there exists such peace that all of these become secondary. They are no longer gigantic and herculean, but are dwarfed by the perfection of peace through the Indwelling Spirit. Once such things were conquerors; now they are conquered.

When peace has come, worry is replaced by worship, fear by faith, hostility by hope, anxiety by assurance. The coming of the Sanctifier has left the once-encumbered man with emancipated mental faculties. Once man is set at liberty, no ensnaring liability need ever steal away the poise of the "Perfect Peace" of the one "whose mind is stayed on thee."

For peace gathers what life scatters. Like the rainbow, the sign of God's peace after the deluge, it hovers over the contradictions of life. The alien is made friend, what was wounded is healed. What was torn is made whole. Even the future holds no fear for the soul that is filled with Christ's peace. Where peace holds sway, time holds its breath.

This is the Christian's foundation for peace: our confidence

The Fruit of Joy and Peace

in God's plan that only death will bring us finally into His presence. So we have an experience of entry rather than departure, promise instead of the ultimate lie, and victory over defeat.

This is different from the world's peace, which is founded on death-escape as opposed to death-embrace: escape by pretending in many ways that death does not exist, that we really aren't closer to it today than yesterday.

All are growing older, no matter how we try to cover it up. Shall we not, as Spirit-filled Christians, tell it like it is?

For everyone, there is an appointment with death. We do not have a choice to die or not to die, or even when, but only how.

Jesus once told a close friend,

I am the resurrection and the life;
Whoever believes in Me,
though he should die, will come to life;
and whoever is alive and believes in Me
will never die.
(John 11:25-26)

How then, is a man to experience peace? Only in choosing the kind of death, being crucified when alive in a death to self-desire that we might come alive to God-desire.

All other ways to peace are temporary. In truth we know that this natural life must end in death, or life—in Him.

Shall we not die now, daily, that we may live forever, with Him?

One of the most beautiful verses of the Bible is the one that delineates peace in the present to the believer, and in the future as though it were already fulfilled in prophecy.

Kindness and truth shall meet;
justice and peace shall kiss.
(Ps. 85:11)

Only God can have mercy and combine it with truth, righteousness, and peace to the sinful, weary heart of man. Only through Christ can we experience that wonderful kiss of sweet peace within our souls. Pardon, comfort, promise, wondrous peace, and everlasting hope—these are elements of the righteousness that is the kiss of peace—the gift of God's love.

But Our Lord does not give us His peace fully and once for all. It is He who, by His Spirit, constantly creates this gift in the members of His body, or, more exactly, He renews it ceaselessly within them, when it has so often been agitated by the passions, or temporarily overthrown by the events of life into which confusion has been brought by sin.

In peace man lives, as much as he is able, that eternal moment in which the Risen Christ takes possession of the glory that He had with the Father from the foundation of the world, so that in His glory He might subject Himself to the Father, "that God may be all in all" (1 Cor. 15:28). This is the perfection of peace, and at the same time the height from which peace forever descends.

For the consummation brought about by peace comes from the farthest reaches—from God, who penetrates our most remote feelings and thoughts. That is the home of peace. It is great as the heart of God, broad as His wisdom and eternal as His love!

12

The Fruits of Endurance and Kindness

None of us lives in the sunshine all the time. Life has its brilliant suns and its sudden shadows. We pass from moments of undiluted joy to times of concentrated grief. We cannot control the "meeting of the waters" where sorrow and joy converge as one stream to flood the soul.

However, "It is not what happens to a person, but his attitude toward it that counts!"

This age-old saying has been helpful in Spirit-filled living. It goes to the heart of the Christian living and brings into play one's inmost self.

Our world displays little patience. There is much sarcasm, bitterness, envy, pretense, and falsity. It is in the midst of these life experiences that one must see holiness—divine love—filling the cleansed heart and determining the lifestyle.

The word *patient* in the Greek New Testament is *makrothumia*. This is translated "patience"—patient, enduring of evil, slowness of avenging injuries, steadfastness, and endurance.

The New Testament usage of this rich term always describes patience—with people but not circumstances. St. John Chrystom said the word is used of a man who is wronged and who has the power to avenge or "get even," and yet refuses to do it!

The word also is used of God in His relationship with man in His self-restraining love. This divine spirit shared with man is the outflow of the sanctified heart.

One does not come to this kind of holy living by some quick, automatic, self-improvement programs! Nor merely by the passing of years! One is brought here through grace by following God's rule and by divine love filling the heart. *Love brings us here!*

When patience is exercised for long periods of time, and adverse circumstances as well as people cause the long, drawn-out pain, patience becomes endurance—the fruit of the blessed Holy Spirit.

A primary hindrance to deep spirituality has always been impatience. Most of us like to see things move. We do not take kindly to frustration and delay. We would like to snap our fingers and have results right now. But life is not like that, and one of the facets of the Spirit-filled life is willingness to wait.

This is described by the term "endurance." It applies to the quality of endurance under pressure. Endurance is not passive carelessness. *It is concern that conquers all adversity by holding steady.* It is the manifestation of a holy and fruitful life lived under bad times as well as good times.

It was the Apostle Paul long before who stated that "afflictions make for endurance" (Rom. 5:3), or, as we would put it, "Trouble helps us learn patience." Someone has said that it is really a pretty dangerous thing to pray for patience, for God's way of producing patience is to send trouble, and most of us think we have enough trouble without praying for more.

Patience always carries with it the idea of endurance, of bearing up with poise and equanimity under pressure. It is actually a form of moral and spiritual power, the strength to meet adversity and misfortune without losing self-control.

It is for this reason that trouble may help us to cultivate patience. Trouble provides the exercise of spiritual muscles. To meet it head on, without flare-up or flinching, is to develop in the Christlike grace of patience.

James puts the same truth in a little different setting when he speaks of temptation as the trying of faith: "Realize when your faith is tested this makes for endurance" (James 1:3). Resisting the attacks of the enemy of our souls, whether those attacks be strong or subtle, develops a perfection of character that cannot be given but must be earned.

Patience is not easy. Indeed, it is one of the greatest lessons the Christian must learn.

To sit quietly when it seems that one should be out walking the streets; to pray earnestly. "Thy will be done," when friends

The Fruits of Endurance and Kindness

encourage us to work out the solution for ourselves; to live by faith when we feel like wringing our hands and when common sense would remind us scornfully that we know not the source of our next meal—these are difficult battles. But the Word tells us that we must "wait on the Lord."

Sometimes God answers our prayers almost immediately (as we usually expect Him to do). We have been thrilled and inspired from time to time upon hearing of such incidents.

But sometimes God tries our faith to see if it is real, and to see how much we really love Him and are willing to trust Him. A saintly lady who witnessed a great revival in England was heard to say quietly but with triumph, "I have been praying for this for forty years." Those years must have seen her burdened through many hours. But think of the blessing that surely flooded her heart when she realized the fruits of her prayers.

Silence is agonizing. And yet, if God does not answer at once in the way that we desire Him to answer, this does not necessarily mean that He does not hear our prayers, or that the answer is a final and definite "No." He may simply be saying, "Wait awhile."

Patience is not learned overnight. It is a spiritual quality that may require years of steady discipline, self-control, soul searching, and prayer. But if this is God's command, we know it must be possible to accomplish.

Wait on the Lord but be careful that you do not yield to the temptation to give up while waiting for an answer. And always expect great things from Him.

We may ask ourselves, "Can good truly come out of sickness, suffering, misunderstanding, bereavement, unexpected loss, and all the blows that bruise the heart?" It did for Job. For after the crisis was past, the man of God said,

> I have heard of you by word of mouth,
> but now my eye has seen you.
>
> *(Job 42:5)*

Good has come out of the suffering of others, too. E. Stanley Jones said: "Paul's letters, mostly written from jail, have enriched the world for ages and will do so in the ages to come. But they could never have been written except in jail. He dipped his pen into the blood of his sufferings and wrote words that are deathless. Through long days and nights of pondering upon Jesus, his thoughts crystallized into immortal phrases through which men have looked into the heart of the redeeming God."

So may our limitations become luminous; our denials can become deliverances. God, it has been said, does not comfort us to make us comfortable, but to make us comforters. Lighthouses are built by drowning sailors. Roads are widened by mangled motorists. Where nobody suffers, nobody cares.

A new world opens up to the person who, in his suffering and trials, senses the possibility of using it rather than bearing it. We cannot explain suffering and adversity, but we may exploit it. Even of the unjust and unmerited imprisonment and trial of His disciples, Jesus said, "You will be brought to witness on account of it" (Luke 21:13).

After all, do we not follow One whose unexplained Cross turned into the golry of Easter morn? The pain of the Cross becomes bearable when we see that the power of God can turn it to redemptive use.

The bruises will come. Job pictures to all of us the insecurity of our life on earth, with respect to its external circumstances. But Job also pictures to us the healing balm of steady faith in One too wise to make a mistake and too good to be unkind.

The Psalmist talks about the "blessed" person "that yields its fruit in due season" (Ps. 1:3). How many times have we experienced rejection or frustration for a time, only to receive later something that made the formerly desired position less appealing.

Since we believe in a God of order, who ordained cycles and seasons and days in divine perspective, should we not commit our days to Him?

In the story of Lazarus we see Jesus confronting impatience. Jesus had learned of His friend's death and chose not to hurry to the grieving family. That He knew and did not immediately respond seemed inconsiderate to the sisters, tortured by the immediacy of their need. Their brother was dead! (Cf. John 11:32.) Martha perceived Jesus only in response to her own needs.

Although Jesus' crying has been interpreted to reflect His love

The Fruits of Endurance and Kindness

for Lazarus, the tears may well have been an expression of frustration. Martha's real need was patience. Jesus must have felt limited by the attempts to confine Him to this world's time clock.

There are times of pain, suffering, loneliness, disappointment that are part of the human experience. Their immediacy frequently is so preponderant that our view of anything or anyone else is obscured. We may long to be rid of the pain and yet not to be able to predict its demise. As Paul noted, "But not only that—we even boast of our afflictions, we know that affliction makes for endurance, and endurance for tested virtue, and tested virtue for hope. And this hope will not leave us disappointed, because the love of God has been poured out in our hearts through the Holy Spirit who has been given to us" (Rom. 5:3-5).

Painful experiences can prepare us for future tasks. Then, years later, if the normal mental and emotional processes have been allowed to work, the recall of the experience is a total and inclusive one and not a recollection of isolated daily episodes.

Occasionally, the nos in our lives are part of God's preventive care. Nos spare us from failure or embarrassment in experiences for which we are not prepared or lack maturity to handle, and from which we might have to pray for deliverance.

There is a point at which we must surrender our temporal time clocks to the timing of the Holy Spirit. While this may require daily adjustments in a time-conscious society, it will pay dividends. Isaiah, writing generations before the "instant age," stated,

> They that hope in the Lord will renew
> their strength,
> they will soar as with eagle's wings;
> they will run and not grow weary,
> walk and not grow faint.
> *(Isa. 40:31)*

Perhaps some of the 120 during the first days in the Upper Room felt that the time could have been used more productively, but after the tenth day those thoughts were abandoned. The

Psalmist reminds us that, when the season comes, ". . . And whose leaves never fade. Whatever he does prosper" (Ps. 1:3).

Impatience makes waiting on the Lord difficult and delays the strengthening of the heart we may need (Ps. 28:14). Impatience and hasty action also may have long-term consequences, as Saul learned after thoughtlessly offering a burnt sacrifice when Samuel was not prompt (1 Sam. 13).

The glory of God's plan includes his final purpose of bringing us victoriously through our tests, to make us like Himself in holiness and in love. If we love Him, and if for His dear sake we face trials and temptations with steadfastness and joy, we may look forward with confidence to the crown of life. To be like Him is our purpose here; to be with Him will be our glory there.

At nightfall, weeping enters in,
but with the dawn, rejoicing.
(Ps. 30:5)

This promise is the invitation to every Christian to abandon the overt acts of impatience. We must learn either to be patient or to suffer from the poverty of impatience and fail to produce this precious fruit of the Spirit.

THE FRUIT OF KINDNESS

As we have seen, the manifestations of the fruit of the Spirit seem to be related basically to love—the love of God shed abroad within the heart of the believer. Love is the source, the impetus, the nourishment, for Christian growth.

"Joy, peace, patient endurance, kindness, generosity, faith, mildness and chastity" (Gal. 5:22-23)—all are expressions of divine love. Where one exists, the others are present also. Included in the list are patient endurance and kindness.

To be patient and kind is to be Godlike. 2 Peter 3:8 implies that God's patience with men grows out of His kindness, His desire to give them opportunity to repent: "This point must not

The Fruits of Endurance and Kindness

be overlooked, dear friends. In the Lord's eyes, one day is as a thousand years and a thousand years are as a day. The Lord does not delay in keeping his promises—though some consider it 'delay.' Rather he shows you generous patience, since he wants none to perish but all to come to repentance" (2 Peter 3:8-9).

The word *kind* has many shades of meaning and often is used without full understanding. In 1 Corinthians 13 it has a wealth of meaning. The Greek New Testament employs the term *chrēsteuetai*. This is derived from the root of the two related words—the adjective *chrēstos*, meaning "useful, good, agreeable, gentle, kind, gracious"; and the verb *chraomai*, meaning "to use, to make use of, to treat, to behave toward." Therefore, a *chrestos* is "one who renders gracious, well-disposed service to others."

It is translated "kind" or "kindness" (Col. 3:12), perhaps coming into English from the German word *kind*—meaning "child." It is a kin-ness or the feeling of love and regard we have for those who are close to us. The feeling that a father has for his child. What is that? The basic idea is to have a strong passion for usefulness—to place oneself at the service of others.

The enduring patience of love is the negative side of service to others. Kindness is the positive side. Origen, the early Church father, held this word to mean that love is "sweet to all."

Every Christian is called into the ministry of caring. It is a ministry that our Lord himself has showed us how to perform. In the Gospels, mention is often made of the kindness and compassion of Jesus. Compassion—empathy—characterized His entire life, and it should characterize ours.

Christ taught us the necessity of compassion in the golden rule: "Treat others the way you would have them treat you in Christ" (Eph. 4:32).

How different life would be, inside the Church as well as without, if these words were taken seriously! But, like so much else in Scripture, they are honored more in the breach than in the observance.

One of the complaints of men in public life who are involved in any sort of debate about moral issues is the number of "hate letters" written in the name of Christ and His Church. The fact is that ugly, angry, sarcastic, and bitter words ill become one who professes the name and nature of Jesus.

It is always something of a mystery how a person may have much light and little love. Yet, more often than we like to think, these qualities seem to go together.

One does not have to compromise the truth or be untrue to his principles in order to be kind. The same truth that is spoken in bitterness and hostility can be spoken in love.

We instinctively feel uneasy about a clamorous, high-strung, unnatural "defender of the faith." As one has said, "The true weapons of the Gospel are not the harsh word and the clenched fist, but the exposed heart and outstretched arms."

There is one thing about the graces of Christian character. They are not fixed and absolute quantities. Like fruit, they grow and ripen.

And the graces of Christian character grow as they are expressed in attitude and action. By being compassionate and kind, by carefully rooting out every fleeting harsh and cynical thought, we develop the grace that so much reminds people of Jesus—the grace of kindness.

Even rebukes, discipline, and correction can best be delivered with kind words. Adequate persons never need unkind words to give authority to their speaking. Kind words come easily from kind hearts, so our first duty is to keep our hearts kind.

> With closest custody, guard your heart,
> for in it are the sources of life.
> (Prov. 4:23)

A common and hurtful fault among God's people is the disposition to "pass judgment" on each other. Phillip's translation on Paul's word on judging in Romans 14 is classic: "To judge a brother is to turn critical eyes on him, measure him with my stick, pronounce him 'wrong' when he doesn't come up to my standard." It seems no one is above falling victim to such treatment. The great Apostle Paul was in disfavor with the

The Fruits of Endurance and Kindness

Church at Corinth, for he didn't fit their pattern. Even Jesus was weighed by the Jews and found wanting!

This persistent fault among Church people is a special temptation to Spirit-baptized people. The ethics of our salvation mean much to us. This is good, but we need to guard our attitudes lest we become judges of others. A judgmental spirit is unkind and creates unnecessary divisions among good people whose mutual love for God should move them closer together.

While censoriousness fractures the body of believers, it also damages the individual who practices it. Spiritual pride, lack of love, suspicion, backbiting, and other un-Christlike traits form a coalition that will scuttle the soul. Any evidence of rudeness or unkindness is a hindrance to the full sway of the Spirit. The very connotation of the word *kindness* rules out failure to be considerate of the feelings of others.

For most of us it takes some years of walking with God, growing in grace, and absorbing Bible truth to mellow our minds sufficiently and give us an understanding spirit.

It is inevitable that an intelligent person will see faults in those with whom he associates very closely. For instance, it is easy to see faults among fellow Christians in a closely knit church situation or prayer group.

But attitudes of a spiritually mature person include accepting people as they are, loving them, faults and all, refusing to give unasked-for advice, showing a great tolerance of humanity and its mistakes, admitting an equal right to exist to those who do not especially appeal to you, and being willing to make such adaptations as you can to the personality of others.

Within any given relationships there are some to whom it may be difficult to adjust. There will be some we prefer to be with, others who make us uncomfortable. But in Christian love we are to accept and love all members of the family and allow each person his right to be unique.

True, it is farther to Calvary for some than others. Some seem to be born with a gentle, tender nature. However, if Christlikeness is to be reached, we must crucify ourselves and let the flow of tender, compassionate love radiate from our lives. *Kind-*

ness is the overflowing of a truly compassionate and merciful heart. And compassion and patience are twin virtues. Both are fruits of the Spirit. Compassion is the soil from with patient endurance grows. Patience demonstrates compassion.

It isn't possible for the Christian to grow the fruits of the Spirit, but he can *cultivate it*. But how difficult to do, so time-bound as we are. Our lack of compassion and patience arises from our overemphasis on the temporary and immediate.

A clearer view of eternity, and the way it invests this very moment with meaning, creates within us a desire to show forgiveness and kindness. Herein lies a spiritual key to cultivating the Spirit's fruit of patience—beginning to see life from God's long view as it relates to ourselves and others.

It was the short view that prompted the same slave in Jesus' parable to demand payment on a far lesser debt when a fellow slave also asked for patience. What a contrast between the shocking judgment of man and the moving sequence of compassion by the Spirit!

It is God who produces fruit in the life of the Spirit-filled Christian. Man's effort is insufficient. Yet God is pleased to effect growth in man by the working of His Spirit. "This treasure we possess in earthen vessels to make it clear that its surpassing power comes from God and not from us" (2 Cor. 4:7).

Earthen vessels, yes! But His Spirit living and working in us enables us to manifest the fruit of kindness and patience. And the degree of our kindness and compassion for others manifests the degree of our consecration to Christ!

13

The Fruits of Generosity and Faith

St. Paul admonishes us: "Do nothing to sadden the Holy Spirit with whom you were sealed against the day of redemption. Get rid of all bitterness, all passion, and anger, hard words, slander and malice of every kind. In place of these, be kind to one another, compassionate, and mutually forgiving, just as God has forgiven you in Christ" (Eph. 4:30-32).

Generosity of spirit and goodness are God's remedy for this peril. For goodness in the New Testament is not a negative quality. It is an outgoing positive piety, a quality of excellence that reaches out to others.

The New Testament has major words for *good*. One of these is *agathos*. It describes the moral quality of rightness or the beneficial results that follow from the right.

The other word is *kalos*. *Kalos* means not only "good" in the sense of *agathos*, but also means "lovely," "winsome," and "attractive." It adds the idea of the beautiful to the idea of the right.

Both terms are used in the New Testament to describe Christian life and character. But the most characteristic use is *kalos*.

The words that glorify our Heavenly Father are *kalos* words, Jesus said (Matt. 5:16). The "fruit" we are to bear is *kalos* fruit (Matt. 7:17-19).

Christians are urged to "prove all things; hold fast that which is good" (*kalos*) (1 Thess. 5:21). The lives we are to live are good (*kalos*) and acceptable in the sight of God our Saviour (Tim. 2:2-3).

The point of it all is, of course, that, while negative goodness is important, it is not sufficient. True Christian character must always have about it an element of the winsome, the attractive, the beautiful.

There is a goodness that is hard and cold. It may be real, but it is repellent. The disciples of the Pharisees (Matt. 22:16; Mark 2:18) are with us yet.

Christlikeness is difficult to define, but is a very lovely thing.

Stanley Jones told of a Jewish Rabbi who perhaps unconsciously but truly witnessed to the universal appeal of the Spirit of Christ. He said, "I don't believe Jesus is the Messiah. I don't believe the Messiah and His kingdom will ever come. But if it should come, I couldn't think of anything higher and more beautiful than that it should embody the spirit of Jesus."

We must test our lives by the standard of rightness. But even more, we should test them by the idea of loveliness.

It is by manifesting the fruits of generosity that we make vital contact with the world around us. It is in this area of our lives that we prove or disprove the doctrine and the experience of the Spirit-filled life to those about us.

If we project an image of holiness that is narrow, bigoted, harsh, and critical we will misrepresent the truth and drive people farther away from Christ. If we present a shallow, cheap, worldly image of the Spirit-filled life, we fail to present the genuine experience properly, and again we do great harm to the kingdom of God.

On the other hand, the Godly life reaches out to others; it inspires and comforts; it gives faith and hope within the framework of a space-age society. Godliness cannot be duplicated by the false and insincere. If we truly live what we teach, then our lives and our message will be relevant to those about us.

When divine love fills the heart of a person within a world of hatred, when real joy fills the life of an individual in a world of sorrow, and genuine peace fills the heart and mind of someone in the midst of turmoil, those about us will eventually see that there is a difference.

When we display patient endurance, generosity, and kindness

The Fruits of Generosity and Faith

in a society that is seething with strife, selfishness, and impatience, it will stand out in all its beauty.

When we show ourselves to be faithful, mild, and temperate in a world that has lost all self-control and thrown caution to the wind, we will point others to Him who is the embodiment of all these wonderful traits.

Life is made up of little things rather than large things. We live more in the ordinary routine than in the extraordinary. The fact that we do not hate or murder people bears little significance in the mind of those about us. Yet when we show forth in our lives the love of God toward all men by being friendly, understanding, and helpful in the everyday things of life, those that are without soon detect a spirit that is different from the world.

To refrain from cursing and swearing may not be noticed so readily, but to speak words of kindness and comfort to everyone will quickly reveal the Spirit of Christ within our hearts and lives.

To refrain from stealing what belongs to another has very little effect in proving the doctrine or experience of Spirit-filled living. Yet, when we are always honest, fair, and upright in our relationships, this will eventually get through to those with whom we deal.

We will be victorious soul winners when we guard closely our contact with God and watch this point of contact with those about us. Then we will be good witnesses to the glorious transformation that is wrought by the Indwelling Spirit in both our hearts and lives.

For generosity in human nature is the reflection of the divine life and love given by the Holy Spirit to those who yield themselves without reservation to the will of God.

Generosity is seen in attitude and spirit as love, joy, and peace. It is seen in action as patience, gentleness, or kindness. It is seen in the whole pattern of life as faithfulness, quiet strength, and self-control.

In its simplest definition, a truly generous heart is Christlikeness begun and growing. It is the joy of belonging to a God greater than the crises of the present world.

In very down-to-earth terms, *becoming like Christ means that* when we pray to have more of His Spirit, we are asking to be more loving, more joyful, more serene, more faithful, more resilient in strength, and more self-controlled.

It also means that one who professes to be filled with the Spirit while being harsh, anxious, impatient, rough, unkind, undependable, unstable, and lacking in self-control, is only fooling himself, or being deceived by a spirit other than that of Christ.

It is still true, as it was 1,900 years ago, that "by their fruits you will know them."

This does not mean that "the fruits of the Spirit" instantly appear full-grown in the character of the Spirit-filled Christian. St. Paul contrasts "the craving of the flesh" and "the fruits of the Spirit" in Galatians 5:1-24. One difference between craving and fruit is that cravings are of the moment—complete. Fruit, on the other hand, grows and matures.

The important thing is to be sure that the fruit is ripening. To be as fickle and immature after a year, or ten years, or forty years, as when a new Christian is a spiritual tragedy of the first order.

The practical effects of this growth in the Spirit will be more pronounced in certain areas in the lives of certain people than they will in others. The individual who has an uncontrollable temper, who "flies off the handle" at slightest provocation, will find that quick and spontaneous reaction cleansed of selfishness and sin. On the other hand, the person who when crossed just goes into a "slow burn" will find his nature cleansed of smoldering resentments and deep hidden animosities by the constant cleansing of the Spirit.

The person who has been prone to bitterness of spirit and harshness of judgment will, when filled with the Spirit, notice a new and deep dimension of life in his personal relations. He will be able to put up with others as God has put up with him. On the other hand, the person whose temperament and moral character were soft and pliable and easily colored by environment will find reinforcement for the moral will and a divinely given independence of circumstances.

Let us bear in mind that what the Holy Spirit fills, He expands. He is the divine wind, the breath of God, filling us, and thus enlarging us. We maintain the fullness by never settling down to a static level of holiness but by *continuously* receiving His infilling.

THE FRUITS OF FAITHFULNESS

The concordance of the King James Version of the Bible lists "faithfulness" as "firm in adherence," while one of the definitions given in the *Comprehensive Desk Dictionary* for "faithfulness" is "*full of faith.*"

Let us reflect a moment on the fact that both "faith" and "faithfulness" come back from the same root. If we are really to put our trust in God, we must be the kind of persons God can trust. If we would have strong faith, we in turn must be faithful. It is both faith and faithfulness for which the Lord looks when He comes to His Church. Faithfulness is one of the notable qualities of the fruit of the Spirit.

In the concordance of the New American Standard Bible, there is another interesting sequence of related words. In this version of the Scripture concordance it looks like this:

"Faith"—*believe,* trust.
 "Faithful"—*trustworthy.*
 "Faithfulness"—*truth.*

Strong words for living!

Careful thought will reveal a distinct connection. *Faith,* or trust in Christ, comes by hearing the *truth* declared *faithfully* by another.

Jesus demonstrated God's faithfulness in living His truth perfectly. In all things, He sought the truth of His Father, and then shared it with His followers. He said:

> I no longer speak of you as slaves,
> for a slave does not know what his Master is about.
> Instead, I call you friends,
> since I have made known to you all that I heard
> from my father.
> *(John 15:15)*

Herein was Jesus' secret of faithfulness, proclaiming daily the truth of His Father. He never planned that it be any different for His disciples. The Spirit's fruit of faithfulness, as Paul knew, takes the cultivation of truth proclaiming to mature and develop.

Jesus' words about the necessity of truth abiding in order to be fruitful are recorded in this same chapter of John:

> If you live in me,
> and my word stays part of you,
> you may ask what you will.
> It will be done for you.
> *(John 15:7)*

What trust He placed in the faithfulness of believers who were to be the possessors of the Living Word, the residence of His truth in the world! He knew that such a Spirit-filled abider would pray, not selfishly, but "in truth": "Thy kingdom come, Thy will be done. . . ." Only in such complete abandon to God's truth in Christ Jesus do we begin to know the Spirit's enabling, which produces the fruit of faithfulness—our adherence to, and the living out of the faith we claim to possess!

Lack of consistent dependability is an overwhelming foe to the life of Faith. God puts a higher value, therefore, on faithfulness than He does on brilliance. Not everyone can be talented, or exercise gifts that receive public praise. But all, whatever their lots or station can be dependable, loyal, devoted, steadfast, and unwavering in their relationship with Christ. So faithfulness appears in the list of the fruits of the Spirit. *Faithfulness is the final proof of faith!*

The Fruits of Generosity and Faith

Here is a quality of life available to all, and it seems like such a little thing. Yet how seldom it is found. For few, if any, of us are faithful by nature. Instead, we are selfish and self-centered—*naturally*. But "faithfulness" is a fruit of the Spirit. And man can't *make* fruit! It is not a virtue we *produce*, but as we walk by the Spirit He teaches us faithfulness—to God and men.

What are the means to this faith? How do we come by faith like this? We come by it largely in two ways. One is prayerful meditation on the promises God has given in His word. "Faith, then, comes through hearing and what is heard is the word of Christ" (Rom. 10:17). After all, what God has said is more important than the way we feel or the way things appear.

The other way we come by faith like this is by acting as if what God said had already come about. T. S. Eliot has said, "The greatest proof of Christianity for others is not how far man can logically analyze his reason for believing, but how far in practice he will stake his life on his belief." As Kirsopp Lake puts it, "Faith is not belief in spite of evidence, but life in scorn of consequence."

And this is true of both the faith of achievement and the faith of adherence. There is faith that ventures forth, and faith that holds on. Among the examples of faith in Hebrews 11 are those who "conquered kingdoms, did what was just, obtained the promises; broke the jaws of lions, put out raging fires, escaped the devouring sword; though weak they were made powerful, became strong in battle, and turned back foreign invaders" (verses 33-34). But we read on: "Still others endured mockery, scourgings, even chains and imprisonment: They were stoned, sawed into, put to death at sword's point; they were garbed in the skins of sheep or goats, needy, afflicted and tormented" (verses 36-37). Yet *both* groups were men and women who were faithful to Christ!

So adherence to our faith not only demands the faithful proclamation of Truth, but the steadfastness to adhere to our faith under the most difficult of circumstances—and this, even unto death!

In steadfastness and trust we shall find that trials and testings are not the end of all things, but the edge of new things. We shall learn to live each day at a time, not carrying tomorrow's load with today's. We shall see that it is not the work of life but the worry of life that robs us of strength and breaks down our faith.

Nor is it necessary that we now understand the purpose of it all. The Bible says, "Through faith we understand" (Heb. 11:3), not, "Through understanding we come to have faith." There are some things we may never understand here on this earth. There are many questions we shall never answer. But a thousand difficulties need not add up to a single doubt. Robert Browning saw it when he said, "We fall to rise, are baffled to fight better."

God does not offer us a way out of the testings of life. He offers us a way through, and that makes all the difference. The untested faith is an unknown quantity. It is when faith is "tried by fire" that the dross of self-dependence and human reliance is burned away and the pure gold of trust remains. Jesus asked, "Why are you fearful, O ye of little faith?" Their faith was not to keep them from being tried, but to keep them from being afraid and cowardly.

Almost everyone has heard and admired the ardent testimony of St. Polycarp, the Christian martyr. When asked to renounce Christ or forfeit his life, he responded, "Eighty and six years have I served Him and He never did me wrong; and how can I now blaspheme my King that has saved me?"

There is little doubt that Polycarp was familiar with the words of his Lord to the Church: "Remain faithful until death and I will give you the crown of life" (Rev. 2:10).

His life and death have served throughout centuries as a clear example of faithfulness. By it many have renewed their convenant with God to be more faithful in their daily living.

St. Paul gave testimony of a faithful life just before he was beheaded by Nero: "I have fought the good fight, I have finished the race" (2 Tim. 4:7).

These instances of faithfulness caused the second-century theologian Tertullian of Carthage to observe, "The seed of the Church is the blood of Christians."

Because these martyrs and others have planted "the seed"

The Fruits of Generosity and Faith

with their blood, each follower of Christ in this age should not do less than be faithful regardless of the cost.

When one considers the tremendous price paid by Christ on the Cross for the redemption of mankind, he must realize that "following afar off" does not meet the requirements of faithfulness. Only a commitment that follows closely and constantly will be rewarded with "the crown of life."

Faithfulness has at least three inherent qualities that cannot be overlooked.

First, it is a mark of discipline and habit. People are not faithful simply because others expect them to be. Rather they choose to be faithful because that is what they expect of themselves. No person is born faithful—he fashions the habit.

Second, faithfulness is a mark of character. Closely akin to discipline and habit is Christian character, which primarily emanates from discipline. If a man is unfaithful, he mars his character, thereby losing his own sense of self-respect as well as losing the respect of others.

Moreover, faithfulness is not a peripheral matter. *Rather it is the heart and soul of Christian character!*

14

The Fruits of Mildness and Chastity

One does not have to be a Biblical scholar to recognize the great emphasis that Scripture places upon the virtue of humility. This should be obvious even to the person only casually familiar with the content of the Bible.

Throughout the Word of God it is made quite clear that genuine humility is not something optional, not something reserved for those who may be deemed especially holy, but rather is necessary as an ingredient in the life of any true child of God. In view of the Scripture evidence, the necessity and importance of humility can hardly be overemphasized.

Moses was noted and commended for his meekness (Num. 12:3). The Lord Jesus began His Sermon on the Mount with a benediction upon the poor in spirit and the meek (Matt. 5:3,5). Paul includes mildness among the fruits of the Spirit (Gal. 5:22-23). The true believer must manifest Christian love, and such love must not be puffed up (1 Cor. 13:4). Peter tells us that God resists the proud and gives grace to the humble (1 Peter 5:5).

The supreme example of humility is the perfect life of our Saviour. This fact, by the way, makes it perfectly clear that humility does not necessarily presuppose personal sinfulness. One has but to look at the life of Jesus to see that meekness is not weakness or spinelessness. Nor is it cast-iron rigidity and unteachable self-righteousness. Though He could truly say, "I and My Father are one" (John 10:30), yet

He was known to be of human estate,
and it was thus that he humbled himself,

The Fruits of Mildness and Chastity

obediently accepting even death,
death on a cross!

(Phil. 2:7-8)

Though "King of Kings and Lord of Lords" (Rev. 19:16), He "came not to be ministered unto, but to minister" (Mark 10:45).

From morn till eve He ministered to the sick and the sorrowing, to the outcasts, to the publicans despised and hated by the self-righteous Pharisees. His supreme aim was to glorify His heavenly Father in a life of perfect obedience to His will.

It has been said that "the reason God is so great a lover of humility is that He is the great lover of truth." Humility is knowing the truth about ourself, while pride is self-deception. Only those who are spiritually blind can be self-important. The Pharisees were proud, boastful, full of self-righteousness, because, as our Lord told them, they were blind to their real moral and spiritual state, "blind leaders of the blind" (cf. Matt. 23:16-24; John 9:39-41).

There is nothing else like a revelation of our true state, and of Christ's redeeming love at Calvary, to bring us low and to wring from us the cry, "God, be merciful to me a sinner" (Luke 18:13).

But the manifestation of humility is difficult. This is clear not only from the nature and frequency of Biblical exhortations but also from a consideration of the widespread lack of humility in our world (including the Church) today.

Of course, many who lack humility profess it. Because of its tragic truth, the hackneyed line about the man who is "proud of his humility" is not funny after all.

Happily there are many thousands of God's people who do see the need of humility and who genuinely try to maintain an unassuming attitude. It is an unhappy fact, however, that many such saints have a false view of what humility really is.

Surely if we accept the teaching of Scripture we must acknowledge that true humility on our part involves the honest recognition that in and of ourselves we are utterly unworthy, that we have nothing to commend us to God, and that we are to follow our Saviour's example in our relations to fellowmen.

Too often, however, God's people demonstrate a false view of humility when they speak of themselves with contempt, or when they deny their talents, abilities, and usefulness.

When called upon to use talents that God has graciously given them, many Christians refuse or beg off by piously denying the possession of these gifts in the name of humility. While trying to avoid being proud and presumptuous, they deny that they can do anything useful, and thus become unambitious, lethargic, and virtually dormant.

This all-too-prevalent attitude is not the humility Scripture demands of us. It is wrong to deny God's gifts even if it is a sincerely mistaken underassessment of one's abilities.

This type of false humility is serious because it is in effect an aspersion on our sovereign God. The denial of the gift is effectively a denial of the Giver. How sad it is when God's people have been graciously blessed with abilities and talents, and instead of glorifying God by their faithful use they insult Him by denying that they have been so equipped—and all in the name of humility!

Not only is God dishonored by such a false view of humility, but His Church and Kingdom are robbed. God gives talents to be faithfully used and developed in His service. Surely we would be amazed if we could know how much more the Church of Christ might have accomplished and could now accomplish if this false idea of humility were eliminated..

Too often Christians also confuse low self-esteeem with humility. The "poor, weak worm of the dust" attitude blasphemes the image of God in human personality—however much the image may be marred by sin. The trouble is, the one who thinks of himself a "poor, weak worm" is all too apt to act like a worm.

There are many people even in the Church who have difficulty accepting themselves for what they are. As a result, their Christian victory is limited and their ability to relate properly to others is hindered.

One would think that those who have the witness that they are "accepted in the Beloved" would find it possible to accept

The Fruits of Mildness and Chastity

themselves. If God has accepted them, why should they not accept themselves?

Perhaps this is the rub. Perhaps it has never really dawned upon them that when they came to Christ they came just as they were, and He received them just as they were.

True, when Christ receives us, He makes some kinds of changes in us. But those changes are changes in spiritual motivation, in action and reaction. They are not changes in basic temperament. And they are not, at least immediately, changes in the structure of personality.

We are not called upon to accept ourselves as corrupt and carnal creatures, bound by sinful habits and accustomed to do evil. It is the purpose of grace to change all that. There is a "new creature in Christ Jesus" that takes away this sort of "old things" and makes all things new.

But we are called upon to accept ourselves in our humanity. We may enjoy free and full salvation right here and now. But final salvation—the ultimate deliverance of our humanity from the secondary effects of the Fall—is "to be revealed in the last time."

Those who have been converted and baptized in the Spirit are still fallible human beings, with all the faults and shortcomings of common humanity. We have treasure, to be sure, but we have it in earthen vessels. And some of the vessels are chipped and cracked!

While we do not now actually practice self-flagellation, beating our bodies with whips or rods to "mortify the flesh," yet many of us spend much time in self-recrimination, blaming ourselves because we are not like someone else we admire, whipping ourselves for faults, failures, and shortcomings that lie completely outside the realm of moral purpose.

As a side effect of not humbly accepting ourselves, we find ourselves unable to accepts others. Beyond the legitimate desire to help others, we spend much time trying to make people over or criticizing them because we can't make them over.

There is a profound depth in the second great commandment, "You shall love your neighbor as yourself." If there is no proper and balanced self-esteem, there is no capacity to esteem others. If we do not accept and like ourselves, we find it difficult to accept and like others.

Let no one take the plea for self-acceptance as an excuse for smugness and complacency. In every area where we can improve the efficiency of our service for Christ and His Church or where we can better our performance as Christian men and women, we must work unceasingly at the job.

But in the areas where we cannot basically change ourselves, or where the rate of growth and change is discouragingly slow, let us try to accept ourselves. No better way to do this can be found than the constant thought that what God accepts, we can accept. What God forgives, we can forgive—even our own stupidity and blundering failure.

And we don't have to wince about confessing our failures and faults to God, to others, or to ourselves. When we realize that neither God nor man expects of us perfection in any other area than that of moral integrity, it takes a great load off us. We can do our best, and trust God to do the rest.

The Lord himself has told us,

> As a father has compassion on his children,
> so the Lord has compassion on
> those who fear him,
> for he knows how we are formed;
> he remembers that we are dust.
> *(Ps. 103:13-14)*

What is badly needed, then, is a true humility, which involves an honest, frank self-evaluation. As Romans 12:3 implies, we are to have a proper estimate of ourselves. We are to think of ourselves as highly as we ought to think; not more, but no less either. In fact, Romans 12 emphasizes the need of a humble use of gifts received by the grace of God. For here is the inherent danger: What may start out as a genuine walk with God can all too easily end up as an ego trip in pastoral ministry.

We must humbly acknowledge that the abilities we do possess

have been given to us by our gracious Lord in spite of our unworthiness. Then we are to utilize these talents in the service of Christ, humbly acknowledging that their ultimate effect and usefulness come also from God's blessing upon them.

A right estimate will be a humble one, which recognizes that whatever good we have is of God. It will avoid the extremes of overrating ourselves and of self-depreciation. Let us not allow a false view of humility, no matter how pious or sincere, to lead us into lethargic inactivity. Let us, rather, serve our God in Christ with a true humility that will redound to His Glory.

THE FRUITS OF CHASTITY

Freedom is the universal desire of the human heart. Robert Frost wrote: "Something there is that doesn't love a wall, that sends the frozen swell under it and spills the upper boulder in the sun." That "something" of which Frost wrote is the desire for freedom.

This desire for freedom is a natural instinct common to all men, for the burden of bondage is a dreadful state. It goes directly counter to one of the deepest instincts of the human spirit. God has made man to be free, and he cannot be happy in any kind of physical or intellectual slavery.

But there is a bondage whose chains are far more painful than physical, political, or economic slavery. It is the bondage of the spirit and soul of man in the thralldom of evil and irreligion.

The Apostle Paul wrote he was a prisoner of Jesus Christ by his own choosing. Many times he said he was a love slave of Christ. Some have asked why Paul chose to suffer for Christ and be a prisoner by choice. Perhaps the question can best be answered by saying that Paul had learned the secret of life. He came to know what so many great philosophers tried to learn, and some did after years of study: there is only freedom in bondage. While this statement seems contradictory, still it is eternally true. The free and happy man is he who is a prisoner of moral laws and codes set down by the Creator. And, Paul says, "The fruit of the Spirit is Chastity."

The Bible is a compendium for behavior and it gives cogent reasons for following the admonitions of God. The reason why there are many temptations, and frustration if we follow them unchecked, is that God has created man with the potential for either great good or great evil. We are not machines programmed for certain responses, but rather free wills choosing the good or the evil, sharing in the consequences of that decision.

Men who boast of freedom to go where they please, do what they please, and act as they please are yet in a bitter bondage. They are unable to break the fetters of sin that holds them captive.

For sin is a tyrant. Paul said, in Romans 6:16, "You must realize that when you offer yourselves to someone as obedient slaves, you are the slaves of the one you obey, whether yours is the slavery of sin, which leads to death, or of obedience, which leads to justice."

Christ preferred to expose Himself to the risk of our sin in order to preserve for us our freedom. And this He has done because He willed we should go to Him as free persons, responsible for our choice, master of our actions, and capable of contract to which we yield ourselves entirely. He desires the gift of love—of love that enables us to act with full liberty.

But liberty is not licentiousness. The Prodigal learned this to his degradation and ultimate sorrow. For there is much more to spiritual freedom than the words by themselves might suggest. *It is a freedom that is found in living within the limits of God's law!*

Chastity however, is not just the outward signs of a well-disciplined life. Chastity (temperance), as the fruit of the Spirit, goes to the heart of the soul and is the very character of man. Thousands of thieves are locked behind bars and sealed off from society. However, they still are thieves who simply do not have the opportunity to commit their crimes against a free society. This is true of other crimes and offenses. The miracle of Christ is that man's character is changed and not just his environment. Men who find Christ are not just locked up, but

The Fruits of Mildness and Chastity

cleaned up, and given a new start where all old things are passed away. *Chastity, then, is the very motive of the soul.* Jesus talked of four kinds of soil in which the good seed fell. Only one soil was "disciplined" and produced fruit. By this parable He says that much depends on us in this matter of living the overcoming life. Paul would add later,

> I do not run like a man who loses sight of
> the finish line. I do not fight as if I
> were shadowboxing. What I do is
> discipline my own body and master it, for
> fear that having preached to others, I
> myself should be rejected.
> *(1 Cor. 9:26-27)*

It is a mistake however, to suppose that temperate living is entirely a matter of rigid rule, routine, and habit; or that its highest exhibition is in being able to determine a course of action for the day and then batter one's way through at any cost. Too many other people and legitimate demands are apt to get trampled upon by that kind of obstinacy. Such self-discipline is too akin to bullheadedness and self-will. There is a vast difference between being a self-willed person and a strong-willed person. Such attitudes may be a symptom of basic selfishness. A disciplined character just for the sake of a disciplined character can be as vain and useless as an undisciplined character.

The end must be a larger usefulness, and to this one aim all the various strands of discipline must be compelled to pay tribute. The self-denial required in achieving temperance, the restraint of impulse, the lashing of indolence are commendable; but ignoring people and their immediate needs in order to protect our idealistic programs of self-restraint is not commendable. For our relationships as human beings must always take precedence over our relationships as automatons.

Jesus indicated the true scope of our freedom while in bondage to Him when He said, "Take my yoke upon your shoulders, and learn from me, for I am gentle and humble of hearts; your souls will find rest, for my yoke is easy, and my burden is light" (Matt. 11:29-30).

A yoke envokes the idea of limitation, yet here it illuminates the way to service and power, bringing sanctification for the Spirit-filled Christian and a bonus of love and help to those he serves. For whoever is led to freedom by Christ is not only master of himself, *he is filled with the masterfulness of the glorified Christ!*

The fruit of chastity is the ability to subordinate the lesser to the greater. Here is the problem of priorities—probably the most crucial problem of life. On its solution hangs success or failure, improvement or degeneration, and in the large sense, heaven or hell. When confronted bluntly with these simple alternatives we know instantly which to approve. We would say, "Yes, these are the supreme values, and to realize them is my supreme goal." The problem, therefore, is not knowledge. The problem is actually giving first place to these values in practical daily living—and this places chastity as a fruit of the Spirit, because without it the believer will not reach *maximum* efficiency in the Lord's service.

Spiritual progress requires a continual renunciation of things of lesser value. Every insight into divine truth involves a conscious laying aside of material things.

When the disciples had brought their ships to land after the big catch on Lake Galilee, "They forsook all, and followed him" (Luke 5:11). When the woman of Samaria drank of the water of life, she "left her waterpot, and went her way into the city" (John 4:28). When Matthew heard the voice of the Master calling he "left all, rose up, and followed him" (Luke 5:28).

It sounds rugged and radical but it is the only way to obtain and maintain spiritual victory. Many still doubt the truth of Jesus' words, "You cannot serve God and Mammon." But following after Mammon, even though it be afar off, invariably leads to leanness of soul and spiritual defeat.

Jesus was not condemning the honest occupation of catching

The Fruits of Mildness and Chastity

fish, or the necessity of drawing water, or the requirement of collecting taxes from the citizens. What He warned against was the "tyranny of things" that consume and dominate the soul. It is the inordinate desire for money or material things that dries up the springs of spiritual power. It is becoming engrossed in the tangibles that we lose our sensitivity to spiritual realities.

The madness of owning things and wrongfully using things and persons without the divine madness of sharing and serving leaves us without a meaningful life. We do not live unless we serve. Personality is more than a salable commodity. Personality is a life in all of its relationships among man, God, things, and values. Personality is a composite of body, mind, and spirit in all its relationships.

It is impossible to calculate the harm that has been done by non-Christian views of the body and its functions. The Scriptures teach that each Christian is to view his body as a sacred temple: "You must know that your body is a temple of the Holy Spirit, who is within—the Spirit you have received from God. You are not your own. You have been purchased, and at a price! So glorify God in your body" (1 Cor. 6:19-20).

The Christian view is that the body is sacred and all of its functions good when expressed within the context of God's will. As a sacred temple, the body of the Christian is God's dwelling place. It is to be dedicated to Him as a whole and in each and every part—hands, feet, ears, eyes, vocal cords, brain—by act of total consecration (Rom. 12:1-2).

The New Testament guideline for the Spirit-filled Christian is that, whether he eats, drinks, works, plays, rests, sleeps, or whatever he does, it is for the glory of God. This is Scriptural holiness in action in everyday living. What does this principle imply?

1. The full acceptance of all the bodily functions as good and desirable when expressed in accordance with the divine plan for our lives.

2. A reasonable and intelligent care of the body, and the cultivation of its powers for the glory of God and the blessing of

other persons. This includes the development of wholesome habits of cleanliness, eating, sleeping, recreation, and work, that Christ may be honored and mankind served.

3. A respect for the bodies of other persons. This means that no function, such as sex, will ever be divorced from the person, the consequence of that being to reduce the person (who in God's plan is always to be *loved*) to the status of a thing-to-be-used. This is always wrong, and is just what Satan desires. God's plan is that we should always love persons and use things; Satan would have us love things and use persons!

4. The cultivation of wholesome habits of self-discipline as regards the body and all of its functions. St. Paul declared, "I am my body's sternest master" (1 Cor. 9:27, Philips). And this self-disciplined chastity will not be simply a matter of ascetic denial, but the affirmation, development, and expression of the body and all of its powers for the glory of God.

Such disciplined sensitivity produces continuing results in the balancing and integration of one's life.

Physical, mental, emotional, volitional, and spiritual factors make up one's personality. It is difficult to establish and maintain a balance of these factors. An imbalance creates a lopsided and irregular life. The establishment of a balance is a lifelong process, and can only be wrought by the guidance and help of the Indwelling Spirit.

A sensitivity to the Holy Spirit will reveal the elements that are out of proportion. Large amounts of God's grace and strong doses of discipline will then make it possible to modify the disproportionate elements in the direction of a more pleasing Christian personality. As the Christian develops a sensitivity to the guidance and direction of the Holy Spirit, he will find himself making the right choices and will find himself at the right time and place more and more frequently.

Thus a disciplined mind and a disciplined body, actually, are but adjuncts of a disciplined and temperate character. Disciplined character belongs to the person who achieves balance by bringing all his faculties powers under control. There are order, consistency,

The Fruits of Mildness and Chastity

and purpose in his life. As a result he has poise and grace. He does not panic, nor does he indulge in maudlin self-pity when tossed by cross-currents.

He rises courageously, even heroically to meet life and conquer it. He resolutely faces his duty. He is governed by a sense of responsibility. He has inward resources and personal reserves that are the wonder of weaker souls. He brings adversity under tribute, and compels it to serve him.

When adversity becomes too overwhelming and blows fall that he cannot parry, he bows to them, but is not broken by them. His spirit still soars. Of course, there is purpose and power in such a life! *This is the Spirit-filled life that is lived under bondage to Christ for the purpose of making man truly free!*

15

The Spirit of Sacrifice

It is the Spirit who produces within the believer divine love and all the other related gifts and fruits. He empowers for service. He brings assurance. He helps our infirmities. He is our Counselor, Guide, and Illuminator. The Spirit's action touches the hearts of those who are receptive and submissive to His gentle guidance. Here the law of grace is in operation. But we should understand that, for any grace to be fully operative in the soul, the soul's full cooperation with that grace is required. The blood of Christ is the source of all grace.

The eternal power of life of the Holy Spirit works through the blood of Christ. Through Him the heart can abide always under the flow and cleansing of the blood. It is the blessed Spirit's influence, through whom the power of the blood of Jesus flows earthward over souls, to heal and to purify them.

It should be seriously noticed that *if the full power of the blood is to be manifested in our souls, we must yield ourselves totally to the Holy Spirit.* We must firmly believe that He is in us, carrying on His work in our hearts. We must live as those who know that, within, as a seed of life, the Spirit of God dwells and He will bring to perfection the hidden, powerful effects of the shed blood of Calvary. We must allow Him to lead us and possess us.

While it is the blood of Jesus, of His life surrendered in atonement, that cleanses from indwelling sin, the power, the efficacy, of Christ's Blood is applied by the Spirit. It is quite Scriptural, therefore, to speak of *the cleansing grace of the Holy Spirit.* For the Spirit's flame is the cleansing fire that burns up the dross of base desires within our hearts. The blood of Jesus is described as an "open fountain to purify from sin and uncleanness" (Zech. 13:1). By the power of the Holy Spirit it streams through

The Spirit of Sacrifice

the heavenly Temple. It is always through the Spirit that the blood possesses its power in heaven and in the hearts of men.

The theologians tell us we are to be sanctified *instrumentally* by the Word of God, *efficaciously* by the blood of Jesus, *conditionally* by faith, and *efficiently* by the Holy Spirit. By this we understand that the Bible is our infallible guide as to the manner we are to go about to seek and find the blessing of Pentecost. The blood of Jesus is the meritorious price paid for its purchase. Faith is the one prime condition we must meet to possess it. And the Holy Spirit is the actual agent for changing, purging, and filling our hearts. Only spirit can change spirit, and that is why we cannot ascribe the efficient agency to anyone or anything except the Holy Spirit.

The precious blood, foreknown from eternity and prefigured in the sacrifices of the Old Law, became a reality at the moment of the incarnation of the Son of God. Biblical blood sacrifices, offered for four thousand years prior to Calvary, were prototypes of Him who was destined "to taste death for all." These oft-repeated rites of the Old Testament economy attained their ultimate fulfillment in the "oblation of the body of Jesus Christ."

The hidden value of Christ's blood is the spirit of self-sacrifice, and, where the blood really touches the heart, it works out in that heart a like spirit of self-sacrifice. We learn to give up ourselves and our lives, so as to press into the full power of that new life, which the blood has provided.

Sacrificial blood always meant the offering of a life. The Israelite could not obtain blood for the pardon of his sin, unless the life of something that belonged to him was offered in sacrifice. The Lord Jesus did not offer His own life, and shed His blood, to spare us from the sacrifices of our lives—no, indeed!—but *to make the sacrifice of our lives possible and desirable.*

The voice of the blood will not speak simply to teach us or to awaken thought; *the blood speaks with a divine and life-giving power.* What it commands, that it bestows! It works out in us the same disposition that was in our Lord Jesus. By His own blood Jesus sanctifies us, that we, holding nothing back, might surrender ourselves with all our hearts to the holy will and service of God.

It is the Spirit of God who is given to man (Acts 2:33) to effect man's salvation. If the blood of Jesus brings forgiveness of sins it is because He has merited the Holy Spirit by that blood. Rightly may we call the blood of Jesus the blood of the Spirit, because this human blood of the Son of God has effected the release of the spirit of man. Thus Peter could cry out on the Day of Pentecost that Jesus had received the promised Holy Spirit from the Father, then "poured the Spirit out on us"; that Jesus had "poured forth" the Spirit in the Pentecostal manifestation of wind and fire (Acts 2:33). The baptism with the Holy Spirit is the birthright of every child of God throughout this age!

The Holy Spirit came to apply to our hearts the benefits of Christ's redemptive suffering. *He exists to act within.* And Christ's goal was man's sanctification. This is plainly stated in Hebrews 13:12: "Therefore Jesus died outside the gate, to sanctify the people by his own blood." In the wisdom of God a participation in His holiness is the highest destiny of man. Therefore, also, this was the central object of the coming of our Lord Jesus to earth, and, above all, of His suffering and death. It was "that he might sanctify his people that they might be holy and blameless in his sight, to be full of love" (Eph. 1:4).

How the suffering of Christ attained this end and became our sanctification is made plain to us by the words He spoke to His Father, when He was about to allow Himself to be bound and sacrificed: "I consecrate myself for their sakes now, that they might be consecrated in truth" (John 27:19). It was because His suffering and death were a consecration of Himself that they can become sanctification—or consecration—for us. How glorious are the results of such a sanctification! Through the Holy Spirit, the soul's intercourse is in the living experience of God's abiding nearness, accompanied by the awakening of the tenderest carefulness against sin and guarded by the watchfulness and guidance of the indwelling Spirit.

From one standpoint the atonement is a finished work: Once for all the Saviour suffered to put away sin by the sacrifice of himself. From yet another viewpoint the atonement is an ongoing

The Spirit of Sacrifice

process of reconciliation, carried forward by the Spirit within the Church. What else can the following passage mean? "All this has been done by God, who has reconciled us to himself through Christ, and has given us the ministry of reconciliation. I mean that God, in Christ, was reconciling the world unto himself, not counting men's transgressions against them; and that he has entrusted the message of reconciliation to us. This makes us ambassadors for Christ, God as it were appealing through us: We implore you in Christ's name be reconciled to God." (2 Cor. 5:8-20).

God's love first manifested in Christ and His Cross, was now incarnate in Paul. Jesus' prayer had been answered: "That they may be one even as we are one." With complete candor and true humility the Apostle could say, "And the life I live now is not my own; Christ is living in me" (Gal. 2:20). Paul had found an identity, not only of life but of mission, with Christ. So much so that he coud write, "Even now I find joy in the sufferings I endure for you. In my own flesh I fill up what is lacking in the sufferings of Christ for sake of his body, the Church" (Col. 1:23-24). *The atonement was moving forward through the sufferings of this Christ-indwelt man.* If we are to fulfill our ministry of reconciliation, to the passion of Christ we must add the compassion of our own hearts.

For the sword that pierced the heart of Jesus brought forth "streams of sweet water"—the Precious Holy Spirit—to satisfy the thirst of a lost and dying world. How needful it was for us that God should permit this incomprehensible suffering! And this brings us to the difficult question of sickness, suffering, and death in the life of the Spirit-filled Christian.

We know that sickness and suffering in themselves have no value. Their meaning comes to them from both a personal and a cosmic historical context. From the personal point of view sickness can be considered as progressive or regressive, positive or negative, according to the meaning conferred on it. Considered cosmically, sickness is a stage of evil in the world in its trajectory toward eschatological harmony, the new earth and the new heaven promised at the end of time. Healing, therefore, is always a breaking in of the resurrection—a taste of the glory that is to come.

Sickness is also a reminder of the precariousness of this life; it is an experience of the diminishment of those biological forces that disappear in death. And so it is like a forerunner of the process that leads from temporal to eternal life. Sickness ought, therefore, to constitute a strong moment in the gradual formation of the self. For if the last instant gives to every life its final, total, and last meaning, *it is because all the preceding instants give meaning to this last moment of human time.*

By death the human person changes to a condition of unalterable achievement. Death is the end of one manner of living and the beginning of another; it is resignation for the body but assumption for the person. With this understanding, hope lights up the night of bereavement and signals the dawn of eternal day!

Christ himself did not come to explain human suffering but to dwell in it, to fulfill it and by that to alleviate it, to replace the need for an explanation by his human-divine presence. The Christian meaning of sickness and suffering is to shape ourselves to Christ's suffering. This is not a natural thing, but the fruits of a faith that declares with St. Paul that the power of God dwells in the weakness of human creatures. But this faith gives meaning to sickness only when the subject lovingly inserts himself into an objective history of salvation, making suffering both redemptive, vicarious, and creative.

This vision of faith indicates that suffering builds up the kingdom to come. Without the eschatological realization of the kingdom to come, we are dealing with suffering only as a *mystery*. In the proper perspective, we are dealing with suffering as a *ministry* as well. This fact shows us that the living human being, sick or not, can aspire to a transnatural form of life. *He can transcend his situation.* This is an essential aspect for a Christian understanding and anthropology of sickness.

Thus the Spirit-filled Christian will always have to try to see better what the sacrifice of Christ means for his own life. For some, the sacrifice of Christ is response; for others, it is a call.

The Spirit of Sacrifice

In the face of this, we have to learn to make the sorrowful aspects of the world a moment of contemplation so that our visions can be enlarged. Suffering, which so easily retires within itself, when transfigured can become a sacrament of charity, an effective sign of opening out of one's self to others.

Suffering disintegrates the body and its functions up to the very point of our individual personalities and finds in Christ a superior level for the integration of our resources and powers. When we achieve this realization, we will no longer find a paradox in discovering behind suffering and sickness a potential for joy and growth—a sentiment in the New Testament that is always found bound to faith and hope in the Holy Spirit—and one that I embrace as my own!

Isaiah saw the Messiah—Saviour—as the suffering Servant of the Lord:

> Yet it was our infirmities that he bore,
> our sufferings that he endured,
> while we thought of him as stricken,
> as one smitten by God and afflicted.
> But he was pierced for our offenses,
> crushed for our sins,
> upon him was the chastisement that
> makes us whole,
> by his stripes we were healed.
> (Isa. 53:4-5)

The inspired prophet also saw the fulfillment and proclaimed it in a portrayal that Jesus applied to himself:

> He has sent me to bring glad tidings to
> the lonely
> to heal the broken hearted;
> to proclaim liberty to the captives,
> and release to their prisoners—
> to place on those who mourn in Zion
> a diadem instead of ashes,

to give them oil of gladness in place of mourning,
a glorious mantle instead of a listless spirit.
(Isa. 61:1-3; Luke 4:17-18)

The sufferings of Christ are unique in that they provided atonement for sin. Therefore the sacrifice of Calvary need not and cannot be repeated. He became the Author of eternal salvation of sinful men, but the crimson stream must be replenished by the poured-out lives of those who have been forgiven and cleansed by the blood of Christ. Paul affirmed, "I fill up what is lacking in the sufferings of Christ." The sorrows of Christ are fruitful only as sacrificial living and giving are seen in the lives of those who have put on the Lord Jesus Christ.

Christ not only bore our sins in His body on the tree; of our sorrows He also bears part. By His grace the Christian's sufferings and grief are sanctified, yes, glorified. To the submissive, trusting soul strength and grace are provided to make him more than conqueror. This is not for the one who turns bitter and cynical in his loss or sorrows. Nor is it for him who wilts in self-pity or becomes a cold stoic with his head bleeding but unbowed. It is for all who find that perfect delight in that God's strength is made perfect in their weakness. Then scars are a testimony that God's grace is sufficient, abundant. And wounds pour out a healing balm to comfort and inspire faith in all who mourn in Zion. "For as the sufferings of Christ abound in us, so our consolation also aboundeth by Christ" (2 Cor. 1:5).

Truly to have a sympathizing God we must have a suffering Saviour, and there is no true fellow feeling with another in the heart of him who has not been afflicted like him. Only the wounded can minister healing to the wounded.

We cannot do good to others save at a cost to ourselves, and our afflictions are the price we must sometimes pay for our ability to sympathize. He who would be a helper, must have first been a sufferer. He who would be a saviour must somewhere and somehow have been upon a cross, and we cannot have the highest happiness of life in succoring—comforting—others with-

The Spirit of Sacrifice

out tasting the cup that Jesus drank and submitting to the baptism wherewith He was baptized.

It has been said that God does not comfort us to make us comfortable, but to make us comforters. Thus our life becomes the hospital ward where we are taught the divine art of comfort. We are wounded that, in the binding up our own wounds by the Great Physician, we may learn to render the same service to the wounded everywhere.

We pray that this realization will give new meaning to the trials and suffering in our own lives, the saddest element in which is often its apparent aimlessness.

For God has a purpose in it all. He has withdrawn His child to the higher altitudes of fellowship that he may hear God speaking face to face, and some day bear the message to others at the mountain foot. And suffering *does* help us to understand the trials of others and fits us to help sympathize with them.

I have experienced in my pastoral ministry that there is a shallow, superficial nature that gets hold of a theory or a promise lightly, and talks very glibly about the weakness of those who shrink from every trial, but the man who has suffered much, or intimately shared the suffering of others—never does this. One who has suffered is very tender and gentle, for he knows what suffering really means. This is what St. Paul meant when he said, "Death works in you." We shrink from suffering, but God sees the tender compassion for others that is finding birth in our souls.

For as we aspire to be one with the Consoler, if we would partake of the priestly gift of empathy, if we would pour something beyond commonplace consolation into the tempted heart, if we would pass through the intercourse of daily life with the delicate tact that never inflicts pain, we must be content to pay the price of a costly education. Like Jesus on the Cross, and Mary, His Mother, beneath the Cross, we must suffer.

So if we have prayed to be completely filled with the Spirit, and to be used to a greater extent in the ministry of the Lord, we should not be surprised or frightened if a wider sphere of suffering awaits us. The divine capacity of sympathy will have a more exalted sphere, for the breating of the Holy Spirit in the new creation never made a stoic, but left the heart's affections tender and true. For the limitations imposed by sorrow and suffering can, if rightly accepted, bring us to a new emancipation of spirit.

It is only when the Spirit of God completely possesses us that we can produce the fruits of the Spirit. Nor is this fruit bearing purely automatic. The soil of our souls must be warmed by the Sun of Righteousness, and watered by the tears of compassion. We must be nurtured by the Word, and pruned by the chastising of the Lord.

And it will take just such a day (or night) of chastising to enable us to listen with a truly sympathetic ear to humanity's groans and sighs. But even suffering is not too great a price to pay for the privilege of touching other lives with benediction. By letting our own hearts be deeply touched by the suffering and needs of others, we go forth to kiss His feet and kneel in faith to touch His garment's hem, and, as we kneel there in the darkness, lifting our heads to shake away tears from eyes that have grown dim, He will come to meet us. One look—a touch of His nail-pierced hands—and we will find our own hearts strangely comforted and expanded. For "he who shall weep the woes of another, shall have wept with God!"

And it is those who are most aware of other people and their needs who most surely touch the hem of God's garments! We do not find God simply by way of our intellectual speculations, but in our sensitivity to others. God is love, and wherever love reaches out in compassion and caring, there God is. Wherever tenderness heals a wound or speaks an encouraging word, wherever concern constrains helpfulness, God is there. Wherever generosity reaches out to bring light into darkness, God is in the midst of us.

For it is with His merciful and redemptive love that Christ associates us to Himself and the members of His Mystical Body, and He desires that we share in the same Charity that fills His Sacred Heart. How greatly would this earthly life be transformed if—amid the sorrows, sickness, injuries, misunderstandings,

The Spirit of Sacrifice

and the injustices with which all of us are sometimes faced—we were willing to undergo the sufferings out of which compassion and mercy, thorough gentleness and a forgiving spirit are born! But we must die before we are turned into gentleness, and crucifixion involves suffering; it is a real breaking and crushing of self, which wrings the heart and conquers the mind.

Unless we are fully surrendered to God, the natural heartstrings have not been snapped, and the Adamic flint has not been ground to powder and the bosom has not throbbed with the lonely, surging sighs of Gethsemane and Calvary. And, not having the death marks of Calvary upon us, there cannot be that soft, sweet, gentle, victorious, overflowing, and triumphant love that flows like a spring morning from an empty tomb.

But when we have passed through the Garden, the Cross, and the Grave, like the Divine Saviour, we can look back and recall the travail of our soul with joy. Indeed, we are no longer afraid to enter into His sufferings, for we are *possessors of the same Spirit of Sacrifice by which we are possessed!*

16

The Spirit of Praise

John 14:13-14, presents a promise Jesus makes to troubled disciples that is almost beyond belief:

And whatever you ask me in my name
I will do,
so as to glorify the Father in the Son.
Anything you ask me in my name
I will do.

At first look the promise appears to have no boundaries. It is absolute, without limits, undefined. But in the Gospel it stands in the midst of a stream of concepts that witnesses to a flow of divine life.

That overflowing life is the work of the Father, carried out by His Son in the world. In fact, it is our ministry of witness to the saving presence of God among men, for as believers we are Jesus' appointed representatives in the world:

I solemnly assure you
the man who has faith in me
will do the works I do,
and greater far than these
Why? Because I go to the Father.
                    (Verse 12)

This life of obedient love to God (verse 15) is the life of the Holy Spirit's presence "in us" as the crucified and risen Jesus returns "to us":

The Spirit of Praise

> I will ask the Father
> and he will give you another Paraclete—
> to be with you always; . . .
> I will not leave you orphaned:
> I will come back to you.
>
> (Verses 16,18)

The Holy Spirit is the life of Jesus in us as a life of prayer, enabling us to continue His mission in the world.

Jesus' promise for our task is that "whatever you ask in my name, I will do." The condition is that we ask in His name.

To invoke Jesus' name in prayer is no gimmick-formula, no surefire mechanism, a kind of magic spell by which we coerce God to give us what we want. Such belongs to pagan superstition, not to Biblical faith. Unfortunately, some of the modern emphasis on the "supernatural" is more akin to magic than it is to miracle.

Rather, "name" in the Scriptures indicates the person as he inherently is. In John 1:12,

> Any who did accept him
> he empowered to become children of God.

Those who "did accept Him" are those who put their faith in the person of Jesus. John 20:31 states: "But these have been recorded to help you believe that Jesus is the Messiah, the Son of God, so that through faith you may have life in his name." Life is the gift of the crucified, risen Christ.

So to "pray" in Jesus' name is to ask in harmony with the moral character and saving purpose of Jesus in the world, "so as to glorify the Father in the Son." To use a friend's name in the course of our everyday affairs is to refer to him in a way consistent with his integrity and wishes. To pray is a holy endeavor.

Jesus' works in the world were the extension of His prayer life. His prayers indicated the unity of His will with the Father's (11:41). In the same way our continuation of Jesus' mission of witness to men depends on prayer. Our mission is the gift and works of the Father expressing His will in the world (John 5:14).

Further, to pray in "Jesus' name" is to ask in compelte dependence on the presence of Jesus:

> the Spirit of truth, . . .
> he remains with you
> and he will be within you.
> (14:17)

True praying is motivated by His life in us, informed by the breath of the indwelling Spirit of truth: "The Spirit too helps us in our weakness, for we do not know how to pray as we ought; but the Spirit himself makes intercession for us with groanings that cannot be expressed in speech" (Rom. 8:26).

We read further that "he who searches hearts knows what the Spirit means, for the Spirit intercedes for the saints as God himself wills." "He," of course, is God. He can read the groanings; He can interpret the sighings. He can tell what the tears mean, and He answers these groanings and sighings because they are in accord with His own mind and will. In this way the Spirit of God helps our infirmities.

It does not mean that the Spirit intercedes up in heaven; Christ is doing that. But, in this body of ours, the temple of the Holy Spirit, He makes intercession, creates desires, and inspires prayers, petitions, and praise.

Therefore, we pray in the flow of the life of Jesus in our world by the Holy Spirit. The Holy Spirit has come to help us to pray, to help us to know what to pray for, to turn our praying into the dynamic process of the work of the Father in His world. Jesus' "in my name" limits our prayer life, but with a limitation that shatters the very word!

Prayer, like all good and great gifts of God, however, is not without its pitfalls. One of the most subtle of these is preoccupation with the negative and limiting side of anxieties and fears. When prayer becomes anxious, fretful, preoccupied with self and

The Spirit of Praise

problems, it may make one weaker instead of stronger and it may hinder instead of help.

A minister who had suffered a complete nervous breakdown, and after a long battle had finally recovered, spoke of a lesson he learned from this experience: "It may be difficult for us at times to acknowledge that prayer can somethimes make us worse. The prayer which focuses attention on our problems can increase it rather than bring the solution."

Prayer such as this is little more than sanctified worrying. It results in the same spiritual and even physical weakness that comes from any sort of anxiety or morbid fretting. It is really praying in fear instead of in faith, in doubts instead of in confidence.

This does not mean that those situations and needs that tend to make us anxious and concerned are not proper subjects for prayer. Far from it. But we must learn the fine art of committing all our care to Him who cares for us. The secret is to "take your burden to the Lord and leave it there."

Still we must never forget that God has given us the priceless gift of prayer through His indwelling Spirit, not only to secure for us the help we need, but also to enable us to become channels of His power to others. Prayer is not a matter of getting for ourselves what we want most. *It is a matter of giving God a means to do what He wants most.*

But prayer may become ingrown and turn back upon the self and its own interest to too great a degree. The Bible sounds a needed caution at this point: "You ask and you do not receive because you ask wrongly, with a view to squandering what you receive on your pleasures" (James 4:3).

Ingrown prayer may dwell on its defeats and brood over its problems until it drains away courage and takes the heart out of the battle. We should never linger unduly in the past, mulling over why things have happened or why situations have turned out as they have. The past is of concern only to be accepted— and to be used as the basis for a wiser and stronger future. "I give no thought to what lies behind," said Paul, "but push on to what is ahead. My entire attention is on the finish lines as I run toward the prize to which God calls me—life on high in Christ Jesus" (Phil. 3:13-14).

Outgoing prayer turns its eyes away from self with its defeats and limitations, and lifts them to the sovereign God who hears and answers. It involves waiting and not worrying. It is relaxed rather than tense. It anticipates victory instead of defeat. It expresses confidence and assurance, not anxiety and dread. *It is more conscious of divine than of human problems.*

It is here, as we linger in His presence, that the Holy Spirit lifts us out of the shallows of self-concern into the mighty oceanic fullness of God's love, and our prayers become prayers of praise and thanksgiving!

And true Spirit-filled living is an everyday affair. It has to happen every day to be valid—in the extreme of life as well as the routines. "The kingdom of God is not a matter of eating and drinking, but of justice, peace, and the joy that is given by the Holy Spirit" (Rom. 14:17).

The thankful heart becomes a victorious heart. Chapter 20 of 2 Chronicles records a great victory for the kingdom of Judah when their land was invaded. The prophets called for singers to "praise the beauty of holiness," and to say, "Praise the Lord, for his mercy endures for ever." Verse 22 records the fact that thanksgiving turned defeat into victory.

The offering of thanks and praise always reflects our confidence in the faithfulness and goodness of God. Moreover, thanksgiving reflects our values of life. If we are self-centered, we fail to recognize God's outpoured blessings, and therefore seldom pause to remember to offer praise.

Thankfulness is a way of looking at life, and it brings its blessings even though it may be difficult. If Jesus could practice thanksgiving in spite of all the difficulties of the day, you and I will find reason for thankfulness in the commonplace routine of our private lives. Thus we shall find ourselves strengthened in spirit to meet the pressing problems that are everywhere. Today my step will be a little lighter because I have said in my heart, "Father, I thank Thee."

The Spirit of Praise

George Herbert was the seventeenth-century British minister-poet who left the Church a rich legacy of devotional verse. In a short stanza he titled "Our Prayer," Herbert wrote:

> Thou that hast given so much to me,
> Give one thing more—a grateful heart;
> Not thankful when it pleaseth me,
> As if Thy blessing had spare days;
> But such a heart, whose pulse may be Thy praise.

The blessing that caps all others is the blessing of a grateful heart.

True thanksgiving cannot be turned on and off like an electric light or a water faucet. One cannot be thankful when it pleases him unless he has learned to be thankful at all times.

Contentment, be it said, does not come automatically with any state of grace. It is something to be learned. The Apostle Paul wrote: "For whatever the situation I find myself in I have *learned* to be self-sufficient" (Phil. 4:11).

Nor is such contentment a passive acceptance of situations that ought to be changed. It is the adequacy of one who draws on resources from above. Whose whole heart beats with the pulse of praise.

We cultivate the spirit of thanksgiving within ourselves when we stop to reflect that God's blessings include more than the special benefits we dignify with the name "blessing." Not some of what we have, but *all* we have, comes from God's good and generous hand.

In the same passage in which Paul speaks of learning the lesson of self-sufficiency, he cautions us to "dismiss all anxiety from your minds. Present your needs to God in every form of prayer and in petitions full of gratitude" (Phil. 4:6).

In 1 Thessalonians 5:16-18, the Apostle wrote: "Rejoice always, never cease praying, render constant thanks, such is God's will for you in Christ Jesus." "Give thanks to God your Father always and for everything in the Name of Our Lord Jesus Christ" (Eph. 5:20). Only those who have learned that God "makes all things work together for the good of those who have been called according to his decree" (Rom. 8:28) can give thanks for all things. It is not that all things are good in themselves, nor that they work together by any power within themsleves. *It is God who works in all things to bring about the final good of those who trust His grace.*

If we are to have hearts that beat with the pulse of praise, we must learn to give thanks for hope as well as for sight. We can be grateful for what God has promised as well as for what He has already conveyed to us.

How often we forget God's blessings and grumble at our blunders, and end up blaming others—or even the Lord! Let us murmur not at the ills we may suffer, but rather thank God for the many mercies and blessings we have received by His hands. He is still the Lord that answers prayer, sweetens the bitters of life, and gives final victory!

Praise to God creates a climate for its growth. Thankfulness unexpressed will soon wither like plants that have no oxygen.

The Psalmist cried, "Let every thing that hath breath praise the Lord." There is a true sense in which all God's works do praise Him. But suns and stars, seas and rivers, mountains and plains, plants and trees, birds, beasts, and fishes praise God involuntarily. The praise in which God delights is that which springs up within the soul of His crowning creation—man. His exultations are those of a creature of intelligence and volition. He knows that every good and perfect gift comes down from the Father of light. Every blessing of life is from God. Therefore a fountain of spontaneous praise should flow from our lips.

> Sing joyfully to the Lord, all you lands,
> break into song; sing praise.
> Sing praise to the Lord with the harp,
> with the harp and melodious song.
> With trumpets and the sound of the horn,
> sing joyfully before the King, the Lord.
> (Ps. 98:4-5)

The Spirit of Praise

"All that is within me, bless his holy name." Hearts filled with arrogance or pride, jealousy or covetousness, hatred or malice cannot call on all that is within them to bless the Lord. Only those who know the blessedness of the meek, the peacemakers, those who do hunger and thirst after righteousness, the merciful who obtain mercy, the pure in heart, and those who love God with all the heart, soul, mind, and strength and their neighbor as themselves, can call upon "all that is within" them to bless the Lord.

The fountain must be pure for the flowing, sparkling waters of praise to pour forth in sweetness. The tree must be good if it is to bear the fruit of righteousness, which is peace. Only those who are inwardly cleansed and filled with the fullness of the Blessed Holy Spirit can see the Lord and worship Him in the beauty of holiness.

Praise, therefore, is both a mind and a mood. It is at the heart of Spirit-filled living and is induced by the grace of God through the indwelling Spirit. Without it the tone of our lives is sub-Christian. Our Christian faith, too, loses its radiance and winsomeness. Conversely, the Christian's joy is made contagious by thanksgiving. The world wonders when the Church rejoices, not when it criticizes and complains.

Praise is also a purifier, for it puts us into the presence of God and cleanses our vision. It turns us from the morbid and keeps us from becoming pessimistic. The thankful heart puts God in control and does not fret about the final outcome of things. Even God's delays do not baffle him unduly, for he is afforded both endurance and divine assurance. The victory of God is always brought near when the heart is lifted in song and thanksgiving.

Someone has well said that "praise is faith in action." It grows out of a settled conviction that God has a wonderful purpose in every providence. It is crippled by every lurking doubt as to His goodness, His wisdom, and His attentiveness to every detail of our lives. The doubts may be in the subconscious mind, but their effect is nonetheless devestating.

True thanksgiving, therefore, must be to the Triune God himself, for until we bless His name, praise has not yet arisen in our hearts. The unthankful and the unholy heart are more than "country cousins"; they belong to the same family.

Any kind of shallow, immature person can rejoice in what is pleasant. The secret of victorious Christian living is to learn to rejoice when many things are hard.

Giving thanks in every situation is evidence of Christian strength, not weakness—evidence of a total reliance on almighty God. Yet true praise is active, not passive. It is the fruit of noble aims, high hope, and wholehearted activity for Christ and others. It is not growing weary in well-doing or giving up. It is persevering whether men give heed or not; being neither disturbed by difficulties, not terrified by danger, not chilled by neglect. It is seeing the rainbow that lurks behind every dark cloud. It is taking time to search for the lovely combination of beauty that is stored for us in ordinary things.

And life—for all of us—is pretty much made up of clouds and winds and dust and shadows, until in the ordinariness of it we may have lost sight of the beauty it embraces. I have watched old people who had experienced life's spectrum of storm and wind, care and sorrow, laughter and tears, hopes and disappointments. In the quiet interlude of their eventide they paused to pray and to remember, and the remembering was lovely. With their prayers at dusk came the glow of the Divine Presence. God smiled upon the underside of their clouds and the whole episode of life became a golden adventure.

Divine love shone upon the memory of their heartaches and draped a rainbow across the shoulders of the retreating sorrows. The tears they had shed through the years began to reflect and to refract the comforting grace and consolation they had received and marked an arching path of beauty where the storm had been. In their eventide tryst with memory, and with God, they quaffed the heady wine of loveliness, pressed from the fruits of the field of living they had tilled.

How much they miss in life who know not how to sit with God in the eventide and watch the light of His love kindle the

The Spirit of Praise

underside of the clouds that linger in the twilight sky! How impoverished are we if we do not by prayer and faith lift the low edges of the cloud so that the setting sun can look beneath and bless our ending day!

Too often our self-pity, our greediness, our anxiety, or our hurry blind us to the waiting loveliness our God provides. We grimly face the night, knowing only that the day has been cloudy and the sun has gone down, leaving the world to darkness about us.

Pity those people who go through life bitterly gathering all the clouds and piling them higher and higher in their memories. They save ugly experiences as squirrels save acorns, that they may feed upon them and nibble at them in the cold, gathering dusk of old age. Then when they are old they have neither time nor inclination to find any new or pleasant experiences to bless their departing days. They must live with their collected memories of chilling winds, stabbing bolts of pain, rumbling thunder of fear, and the passing footfalls of people they distrust. What a pity! What a sense of waste! *They have missed the glowing sunset but cannot escape the falling night!*

Even in the Spirit-filled life there will be some ugly clouds. Each life must have its encounter with tempest and tumult. Only cowards and fools would hope to escape them, but wise persons will plunge into the midst of the storm, questing for loveliness and finding it by the grace of God. Holding His hand, we can go into each day to capture the memory of some kindness, the fragrance of some act of love, the adventure of some new truth, and the excitement of a great discovery. Only then can we return at eventide to sit with Him in pleasant reminiscence, fondling our memories before we go to eternal sleep.

Those who come, in fellowship with God, to close of day will find the setting sun kindling their sky and setting every vagrant cloud aglow. The glow will reflect upon their own faces and upon the people about them. It will fall upon the still waters before them and warm them, and upon the marble-studded field to which their loved ones will bear their mortal clay to plant it and cultivate lovely memories of them.

Today we live. The day will not be long and the setting sun cannot be delayed; all will have clouds in the sky, but not all will have a lovely sunset. All will have memories, but not all will have pleasant memories. Each of us will close his book and go to sleep, but the memories we fondle will differ, and the persons we become will differ according to what we have made of life's short day. What a sunset these clouds will make if we but invite God to come and kindle the underneath side of them with the light of His countenance!

So, in everything give thanks now. We may not understand the way of suffering, loss or tragedy, but our courage is reinforced as we find that through all these things we can gratefully say with the Apostle Paul, "But thanks be to God who has given us the victory through our Lord Jesus Christ" (1 Cor. 15:57). Indeed, the continual sacrifice of praise that God commands delights Him no end, opens a new fountain of joy for us, and blesses everyone around.

Yes, Praise and Thanksgiving are the marks of a Spirit-filled life—a life that has been submitted TOTALLY to the Lordship of Jesus Christ, a life that is completely in the hands of the Lord, a life that communicates daily with the Father and experiences neverending Peace! "Give thanks to the Lord for his loving-kindness endures forever" (Ps. 136:1).